ACTIVATE
HUMAN CAPITAL
A NEW ATTITUDE

RICHARD N. MORRISON

ARCHWAY
PUBLISHING

Archway Publishing books may be ordered through booksellers or by contacting:

Archway Publishing
1663 Liberty Drive
Bloomington, IN 47403
www.archwaypublishing.com
1 (888) 242-5904

Because of the dynamic nature of the Internet, any web addresses or
links contained in this book may have changed since publication and
may no longer be valid. The views expressed in this work are solely those
of the author and do not necessarily reflect the views of the publisher,
and the publisher hereby disclaims any responsibility for them.

Any people depicted in stock imagery provided by Thinkstock are models,
and such images are being used for illustrative purposes only.
Certain stock imagery © Thinkstock.

ISBN: 978-1-4808-4067-6 (sc)
ISBN: 978-1-4808-4068-3 (hc)
ISBN: 978-1-4808-4069-0 (e)

Library of Congress Control Number: 2017900665

Print information available on the last page.

Archway Publishing rev. date: 07/12/2019

This book is dedicated to the memory of Dr. Wilma Stricklin, an inspiring Professor of Management at Northern Arizona University from 1967 to 1976—then professor, chair of the management department, Associate Provost, and Vice President at Northern Illinois University.

FOREWORD

SO YOU THINK you are or you want to be a leader of people. The book that you hold in your hand is your road map to making a tremendous difference in your world. Properly implemented it is a timeless people-focused guide to your success as a leader.

It's not about a specific generation, class, sex, race, ethnicity, orientation, or culture. It's about people. It gives you eight simple principles that meet seven basic human needs.

In each chapter Richard has provided an opportunity to make a difference in the lives of the people you encounter every day. When you take the time to implement these principles, you take the time to make a difference, and at the end of the day, making a difference is what it is all about, isn't it?

Without people, there would be no need for business—who would purchase your goods and services? Without people, there would also be no business—who would provide your goods and services? Who could decide upon how to make the match between what is desired and what is produced? Do you want to make a positive impact on the bottom line of business as well as your life? This book will help you do that.

This book takes you back to basics. Make a positive difference in the lives of people you work with, and you will make a difference in your life as well as the career you have chosen. Employ these principles, and you will meet the needs of the people above you, below you, and beside you. In doing so, you will make a difference in the world you serve.

While the genre of Richard's book is business, the message is timeless and universal. The potential applications are endless. These eight simple principles applied will also make a difference in your family, your community, your organizations, your church, and your own life.

Read on, become people focused, and make a difference in the world.

Pamela Wilson
IT Project Manager

ACKNOWLEDGMENTS

I HAVE BEEN encouraged by everyone with whom I talked about the ideas in this book; all of them thought I should write this book. As my ideas were explained, people became energized and excited by the vision presented in these pages. Therefore, as perhaps with most books, many people have contributed their ideas, the benefit of their experience, their visions for a better workplace, and, in some cases, referrals to others who should be interviewed. To all of them I offer heartfelt appreciation.

Special thanks go to Pamela Wilson, a former human resources professional and current Project Manager for an information technology firm who served as a consultant and guide, and to Lisa Schnebly Heidinger, a published author in her own right, who made material contributions to the content of this work.

From the development of the vision for this book, Pamela Wilson offered invaluable assistance by linking my vision for this book to the actual needs and desires of human resources professionals in the workplace. Pamela encouraged me to consider the continuing education requirements of human resources professionals and to participate in symposia and courses offered through such organizations as the Human Capital Institute and the Society for Human Resource Management. Her consulting on the book was also informed by her work experience in the human resources field and by her fierce conviction that the principles emphasized in this book are both important and necessary to maximize employee productivity.

Lisa agreed to help research and document the experience of academics, business executives, rank and file employees, executive coaches, and others who should be interviewed. She personally conducted interviews and then reported her findings. Lisa also helped my team process the ideas and data already published in volumes of books, academic journals, and popular press articles in order to corroborate the importance of the ideas contained in this work and to differentiate the compilation of these ideas from books and articles already available to the business world. In the process, she offered valuable advice about meeting the needs and the desires of the typical reader. Any failures on my part in meeting those needs are entirely the result of my own choices and are in no way attributable to Lisa's advice.

Ambassador Barbara Barrett, Past President, and Edward Reilly, current President of the American Management Association, encouraged the project and emphasized the importance of passion for it. Jim Hunter of PeopleBest explained the current capacity and limitations of big data in predicting performance on the job. Amy J. Doyle and Toni Weitenhagen-Owens offered valuable insights into the use of analytics in assessing employees' potential. They also encouraged me to examine the importance of motivational influences and goal-setting on human achievement. Julie Morrison contributed the title of this work and conducted research to find proof that implementation of People-Focused Principles of Management produces the desired result on the job.

Finally, I am deeply grateful to Billie Fidlin, Tracie Witts, Laura Gallaher, and Andrew Bernier for their thoughtful comments and editorial advice in shaping the final product.

Richard N. Morrison

CONTENTS

INTRODUCTION

Do what you can, with what you have, where you are.

—Theodore Roosevelt

THIS BOOK'S MISSION is to activate human capital. It does not assume an employee is doing nothing at the moment. It does assume almost every employee could be doing more and would gladly do more given the right set of circumstances. This book is about creating those circumstances. What I discuss in this book is so basic, so fundamental to human relationships, you would think everyone would not only understand what I call People-Focused Principles of Management but follow them instinctively. It should not be necessary for me to write this book. Unfortunately some, perhaps many, managers do not follow all the principles, and often the principles they do embrace are not practiced consistently and do not contribute to an increase in employee productivity.

To help illustrate why I wrote this book, I recently told a story to a group of women who meet monthly to discuss common interests, and of course some of those interests relate to their experiences in the workplace. I shared with the group that I practiced law at three very fine law firms in Phoenix during my career. These law firms were filled with some of the finest lawyers in town, and they were justifiably proud of their firms. Even so, these lawyers were guilty of at least one significant oversight. In my experience, I did not learn of a single occasion in thirty-nine years of practice in which the lawyers authorized employee conferences where this might have been said to employees who were not lawyers: "This is the time we have set aside to ask about your professional and personal goals for your time here and to discuss how we can help you achieve those goals." It never happened. At the end of my story, I noticed the women in the group were looking at each other and nodding in agreement, recognizing the problem at hand.

I see the business challenge of our time is to activate human capital in ways that help employees experience personal fulfillment while serving their employers' business purposes. In this book, I've set out to prove that using People-Focused Principles of Management will increase productivity and profitability for the employers involved, and I've included data to support this. Also, I use the term *human capital* in its best possible meaning. For me, human capital is a conscious reference to the fact that all types of human institutions are required to make an assessment of their assets, to value them appropriately, and to use those assets in the performance of the organization's mission. Managers have an opportunity to demonstrate to the world a new kind of "best management practice," one that values our human assets even more than the financial resources we routinely manage. The wealth needed by a company to fulfill its mission of producing a good or service is commonly known as its "capital." To you and me, it is money. A company must have money to survive. However, I am inviting my readers to see the human (i.e., human capital) as even more valuable, as is the money needed for operations. With that attitude in mind, properly managing the human assets of our organizations should be among our highest priorities.

Activate Human Capital is a call to recognize that people will make themselves more valuable to a company if they feel they are valued by the company.

This book is also a call to action. It is less about the nuts and bolts of how to change and more about being willing to stand and say, "You could be doing more." The surprise here is that managers are not doing what they have been taught. What I say here is what has been taught, at least in a general way, to multiple generations of business school students in the United States and elsewhere. For the last half century, college textbooks on management have taught the importance of valuing the human assets of a business and of managing those assets appropriately. And yet we look around and rarely see it practiced.

While some of the principles mentioned in this book have been explicitly mentioned in textbooks, up until now you could not find all of them in one place. I've scoured texts and have not found them together, rather scattered as disjointed ideas. Instead, they should be grouped together as a prescript for basic management practice.

My first objective is to prompt business managers to look in the mirror and reflect on how they manage. My further objective is to start a conversation by inspiring business leaders and managers to manage people, not positions. Ultimately, this book should produce a different kind of thinking, perhaps with a different language about managing people. It is this change in thinking that will create the behavior change needed to activate human capital.

I often hear discussions about the need to change corporate

cultures—to put more emphasis on people-focused leadership. On the other hand, some effective Human Relations Department directors say, "Forget changing cultures. Change behaviors." I like the distinction, but I also believe that changing the culture can and should lead to changing behaviors. The most appropriate change in corporate culture will come from a change in the attitudes and intentions of managers toward those who are managed, which will result in a change of attitude of the employees toward the managers. Employees should not be viewed as problems because they could be expensive, bring their problems to work, sometimes fail to come to work, or perform functions that can be automated. (I should note, most employees don't all do all those things … in most cases, perhaps, none of these descriptions apply.) For optimum profit, engagement, creativity, and success, employees should be viewed as creative, imaginative, problem-solving agents. They can and will be all these and more if properly motivated and managed.

With this book I am asking some hard questions. Why is it managers have been taught to value the human assets, but in practice this training is largely given lip service? Is it because in college textbooks the usual mention about motivation and leadership of people actually fails to give an adequate explanation about how to do it? Have managers even been taught that People-Focused Principles of Management are in their own best interests but have not been convinced? Or is it simply because the day-to-day operations have left no room to nurture our most valuable resource—our people?

Well-intentioned managers believe their values are correct, and they are fulfilling expectations, often under very difficult circumstances. They may be dealing with hiring freezes, streamlining operations, and doing more with less. At the same, they may also be focused on labor costs, under pressure to get more productivity out of their subordinates, or resisting the temptation to hire more workers until customer demand increases. This book will show how to manage effectively under even the most trying of times.

Why does financial management get so much more attention at almost every level of business than managing the human resource? Why do so many managers say they don't have time to engage with their employees? What is it about measuring performance according to usual business metrics that squeezes the life out of an employer's relationship with an employee? Ultimately, all business is about relationships, and this includes the relationship between an employer and its employees.

To demonstrate how disconnected this relationship can be, the results of a Rasmussen Reports LLC survey found 92 percent of managers said they were doing an "excellent" or "good" job managing employees, but only 67 percent of workers agreed. An additional 23 percent said their boss was doing a "fair" job, and 10 percent found their manager was doing a "poor" job. Another instance of this disconnect had a retired executive recalling when he was at a management seminar at IBM, and the entire management team gave themselves glowing ratings. Then they read their employees' ratings of them and discovered they rated them very poorly. Management had to reassess, readjust, and rebuild.

THE PEOPLE-FOCUSED PRINCIPLES OF MANAGEMENT

The People-Focused Principles of Management I recommend are as follows:

1. Give people a purpose.
2. Communicate widely.

3. Accommodate/manage change.
4. Create a culture of worth.
5. Create a culture of hope.
6. Reward performance.
7. Create a vision of participation in determining the future of the company.
8. Express gratitude.

Properly done, managing according to people-focused principles will improve all business relationships, and in so doing improve efficiency, productivity, and profitability.

The format of this book is to define people-focused management in terms of the values that motivate people to want to do the work that is given them (and more than that, actually—to initiate work because they see how it will contribute to the business purpose). I will introduce each principle, link it to a component of human fulfillment, explain it based on research and lived experiences, and then discuss what it looks like in the workplace.

A word here about why some of you will not act on this: you will be afraid. Fear is a powerful human motivator and the enemy of change. What if people don't respect you or see you as weak when you are kind? What if they take advantage of you and your boss blames you? What if employees become full of themselves and make unreasonable demands?

I will show in the following chapters that research and experience do not support the theory that negative results will occur from following my principles, at least not to the degree managers fear. In fact, the reverse is true: employees who feel valued, respected, and encouraged are determined to work harder to please the manager, whom they now see as an ally rather than an opponent. Though, you don't have to take my word for anything. People-focused management has been done, is being done, and will be done more often as more business leaders comprehend the potential in that form of leadership.

Reading this book doesn't imply you are managing poorly. A gifted honors teacher constantly pointed out to students that anything ever done, from building an airplane to writing a sonnet, could be done even better. The idea that you can do something more effectively is not an indictment of your current practices. I am speaking to everyone from the lowest common denominator on up. You may already be almost at optimum business practice, and a small tweak is all you need. Please bear that in mind as you read ahead.

Throughout this book you will read references to persons and situations. Some of them are identified by name while many are not. In some cases, the individuals interviewed requested anonymity because of the sensitivity of the situation created by their criticism of their own managers. In all cases, named persons have either been interviewed personally or described in published material found in the public domain. All data utilized in the text was found in published material, except as it appears within a quote attributed to an identified source.

HERE'S THE PROBLEM

If you want to teach people a new way of thinking, don't bother trying to teach them. Instead give them a tool, the use of which will lead them to new ways of thinking.

—R. Buckminster Fuller

WE ALL WANT our employees to be energized and committed to their work. That requires a certain amount of personal fulfillment, which I will discuss throughout this book. If work is fulfilling as well as productive in the business sense, employees are much more likely to be happy at work, and the result of that is likely to be increased productivity and profitability for the employer. Frankly, it would be absurd not to shoot for maximum performance in productivity and profitability.

Many employees have told me their businesses are not managing for maximum employee productivity, and in some cases, this has translated to employee unhappiness. Employees want to matter to their employers as much as they want to matter to their family, friends, and communities.

I thought about naming this chapter "Your Employees Hate You. Do You Care?" While it is not likely to be that bad in most workplaces, you may want to ask yourself this question: How many people do I know who are happy at work? If you are like me, your answer may be "Not many." You may be unhappy yourself. How or why does this happen?

Of course there can be myriad reasons why employees might be unhappy at work. Maybe their work is physically demanding and it wears them out. Maybe their work requires long hours and leaves them largely without a personal life. Maybe there is a personality conflict with a colleague. Maybe they feel they deserve a private office but have been given a cubicle. Maybe they are in management and have more work responsibilities than they can perform well. Even CEOs may be unhappy because no one understands their problems, not even their boards of directors. A CEO may also feel isolated without an immediate peer group for evaluation and reflection.

Are any of those things really fundamental to people's happiness or unhappiness at work? What is fundamental is whether their human needs are being fulfilled. Within the world of work, when people are ignored, taken for granted, stuck in a position with no opportunity for advancement, underutilized, underappreciated, or—worse—bored, they are unhappy. There is an emotional response of feeling unfulfilled.

I submit to you that humans have seven fulfillment needs:
- the need to love and be loved
- the need to belong
- the need to express themselves and be heard

- the need to grow
- the need to share
- the need to find meaning and to matter to others
- the need to change

With the exception of the need to love and be loved, I believe people should anticipate that all the other needs identified will be fulfilled in their work, at least to some degree.

When work doesn't seem to matter, things go off the rails. It never changes, it stifles creativity, it blocks new ideas, it isolates people into work silos where few people know what others are doing or why, and there is no apparent professional track to it—no obvious way to develop professionally, to assume more responsibility, and to advance in compensation or to receive other rewards signaling management's recognition of a job well done.

When large numbers of people are unhappy in a workplace, management has probably failed them in some way. It may also be they are being managed by someone who shouldn't be a manager. For example, a manager who does not have good interpersonal skills probably shouldn't be a manager. A manager who doesn't want to be bothered probably shouldn't be a manager. A manager who lacks leadership skills probably shouldn't be a manager. A manager who just wants to analyze his or her department's present and future performance using business metrics probably shouldn't be a manager.

In some cases, managers just aren't ready to manage people—they haven't been educated in management principles and practices. In other cases, managers have been promoted because they have mastered a technical skill or because they are considered the best at something—usually involving an understanding of the financial implications of business decisions—but in reality, they are simply top producers. Or maybe they were promoted because they have the most longevity in the department.

From both a practical and philosophical perspective, it is important that people have the opportunity for fulfillment at work. Unfulfilled adults who spend 50 to 70 percent of their waking hours at work may reach retirement feeling not only that their careers were a waste but sometimes that even their whole lives were a waste—at least to that point in time. No wonder so many people look forward to retirement; many of them still want to find something meaningful to do, and retirement seems to be the context in which that may be possible.

We know management can do better than that, both by utilizing human capital more productively and by giving employees a real opportunity to experience fulfillment at work.

Robert Greenleaf's *The Servant as Leader*, written in 1972, identified a test by which to measure the meaning and effectiveness of the servant leader: "Do those served grow as persons; do they, while being served, become healthier, wiser, freer, more autonomous, more likely themselves to be servants? And what is the effect on the least privileged in society; will they benefit, or, at least, not be further deprived?"

We seem to be living in a time when management of the financial resources of an enterprise is given more attention than management of human capital.

For decades now, business majors have been taught to value human capital and to make sure all employees understand the system in which they are employed so their own contribution to the end result is obvious and they are motivated to take ownership and pride in the result. However, although managing human capital effectively is expressed in words, it's not backed by deeds in many, if not most, workplaces today.

All of this was on my mind when I spoke to the graduates of the W. A. Franke College of Business at Northern Arizona University's commencement in May 2015.

Below is what I said to these graduates, many or most of whom may soon have management responsibilities and more importantly, may have even more management responsibility over the course of their careers:

> In her installation speech on April 23, President Rita Cheng remarked that NAU has evolved while maintaining a person-centered approach. It is an appropriate posture for you, too, as you make your way through your respective futures. Keep that people-focused approach. I attribute my success in leadership to a care and concern for the world—its conditions and its people. In general, people will not respond to your leadership until they know you care about things that are important to them too.
>
> …
>
> In every job and in every workplace, it is people who make you successful. It is people who will act as mentors, managers, colleagues, teammates, supervisors, and staff—and this is important because it's as people that we differentiate ourselves and grow the relationships that make the difference in creating opportunity for personal and company growth. I can look at dozens of résumés and be very impressed by all kinds of skill sets, but what's going to make the difference to me, in who I hire or who I partner with, is the

person's genuine interest and authentic desire to help me and help others achieve what we're all there to do.

Likewise, many times it's as people that we determine what will be successful and what will fail. One concern I have about workplaces is that we are giving less and less attention to utilizing and developing the capacity of the people who work there. The profit motive has led some managers to disregard the human costs associated with impersonal decisions made in the never-ending pursuit of increased efficiency. I believe everyone studying principles of management has been taught to value the asset represented by each employee, but financial management gets more attention. I think Whole Foods CEO Walter Robb is onto something in viewing people as the heart and soul of his company. My advice is that you go into the business world with as much commitment to the human-resources side of your business organization as you make to financial management, for the most underutilized resource in business today is the human person.

...

Remember to consider the impact of your decisions on those who depend upon you. Think about that, and utilize NAU's people-focused approach to it all. It will serve you well.

My remarks emphasize a people-focused approach to management, but there is also the section expressing concern about the erosion in our collective commitment to business ethics. In fact, the lack of commitment to ethical business standards may also bear on the phenomenon of managers who lack commitment to the welfare of their employees, for if the root cause is a character defect in both cases—a basic me-first attitude—it cannot be surprising that employees are frequently disregarded altogether so long as they get their assigned work done.

The character issue is relevant for another reason. There appears to be a pervasive problem among business students—cheating! It is partly cultural-experience based. Students in our universities almost universally report having witnessed cheating in the secondary schools out of which they came. But, there is something about these business students we should understand better. University officials surmise, perhaps without knowing for sure, that students' exposure to cheating on the secondary level seems to have conditioned them to accept cheating as acceptable behavior. I have learned of research finding that business students are, in fact, more likely to cheat while in college than students declaring other majors. What would explain this? Are business students even more eager to succeed financially than other students? Are they just instinctively more competitive than other students and fear they can't compete successfully without cheating? Or perhaps the most compelling of all, do they sense that business is where you can take shortcuts, reap rewards, and get away with rule violations?

People who don't care about others have a problem stemming from a character flaw, insensitivity, or lack of awareness. They want the credit but may never have developed the actual arts of compassion or empathy. "I need to make my superiors think I'm doing a good job but don't have to care about people below me."

There must not be any room for this detriment of character among those who would manage people. Employees want and need to trust their supervisors, but that will only happen if the managers connect with people and build trusting relationships.

Dean Craig Van Slyke of the W. A. Franke College of Business at Northern Arizona University writes extensively on the importance of trust-based leadership, an effort I heartily endorse. Studies show productivity increases where employees trust their managers (Seppala and Cameron 2015), but trust will not develop where managers are unethical, uncaring, unfair, unappreciative, unresponsive, or irresponsible. So character matters, especially if the whole enterprise depends upon management to establish a culture that values employees, inspires their loyalty, and promotes increases in employee productivity and efficiency. I am stressing the importance of character here, but basic character is linked to intention in such an important way. If it's all about what you can do for me, that's a poor attitude. We are so critical of that kind of attitude being evident at work, as well as "What have you done for me lately?" Managers need to care about their people. And the good news is that attitude can be changed. You either have the intention to "do good" or you don't; you may have a cynical attitude. The intention one brings to any human relationship is critical. And the relationship is reciprocal. Good intentions can actually improve poor character over time. On the other hand, poor character can undermine good intention. A company culture upholding the values that translate to good character and good intention will activate human capital.

PEOPLE-FOCUSED PRINCIPLES
OF MANAGEMENT

The very essence of leadership is that you have to have vision. It's got to be a vision you articulate clearly and forcefully on every occasion. You can't blow an uncertain trumpet.

—Father Theodore Hesburgh

BY "UNCERTAIN TRUMPET" (in the quote from above), Fr. Hesburgh suggests that if you don't know what to do when you raise your instrument, you won't make music. You're not going to accomplish your proposed goal of motivating and managing people if you don't know how to.

The eight People-Focused Principles of Management I describe in this book *work*. They produce results, and I will provide insight into how and why they work. In emphasizing these principles, I am not arguing against managing financial resources. Nor am I asserting that managing human capital is more important than managing financial resources. Rather, I argue that managing the human capital is *as* important as managing the financial resources of the firm.

In fact, a very successful advertising man I know about, Bill Lavidge, asserts that one of the biggest lies in business today is "do what you love and the money will follow." He says he would have been a rock star were that true … but no one wanted to pay him to play guitar. He found out he was good at advertising, and then he realized he liked it. By working hard in the field, he rose to the top. Further, Lavidge asserts that you must care about the bottom line. If the profit margin is not sufficient, you can neither reward your people nor expand your business. Agreed. What I am saying is that you actually make *more* profit when you care about your people. Surprise! By caring you get to be a more successful leader of people, and you make more profit for your company.

The idea behind People-Focused Principles of Management is to think of the people before thinking of their function within an enterprise.

Before introducing the principles, I want to recommend a basic approach to dealing with people—all people, anywhere. It is an attitude that undergirds the successful integration and implementation of the principles outlined in this chapter. It is the basic attitude of goodwill. Goodwill has some attributes of kindness, friendliness, and respect, but really no one, two, or even all of these synonyms are sufficient to describe what is required. My approach depends upon intention, not upon personality. Goodwill allows people to meet each other "on the same level," even though they may occupy very different places on the organizational chart. Goodwill gives another person a chance to speak, an opportunity to be heard. Goodwill allows for the possibility that another person may have a really terrific idea, or at least a better idea. Goodwill values other people in the organization for their contributions. It does not require you to like someone. It does not require you to favor someone. It does not even require compassion for another person (although compassion is highly desirable). By itself, goodwill is just a way of meeting another and appreciating that person's role in the organization. Whatever that role may be, it is important and should be acknowledged. Goodwill sets the stage, and it is important. However, in the beginning, if managers do not already possess a basic propensity toward goodwill, developing it will require a new intention.

To be most effective, managers of people need to possess goodwill. After decades of work in the military and in the private sector, I believe I witnessed more goodwill on the job in my military experience than in my private sector experience. This is something of a surprise to me because in the beginning, at least, the transition to military life required submission to extreme disciplines and punishments as a way of conditioning people to following orders. After moving into operational units, I saw that military leaders demonstrated high levels of concern for the wellbeing of their subordinates; they incentivized performance well and often with promotions, medals, and praise; they actively counseled their personnel about possible career paths; and the camaraderie that developed between senior and junior personnel was palpable—though boundaries were still respected. In short, I saw lots of goodwill among leaders in the military. It is a surprise and a disappointment that I have seen less of it in civilian life. In discussing this phenomenon with certain professors of management, I learned it is widely recognized and well documented within academia that the military is quite successful at managing people. In fact, a recent experience strongly suggests that the military is still doing a better job than private industry in investing in people. On May 11, 2016, Vernon Clark, who became the twenty-seventh Chief of Naval Operations on July 21, 2000, spoke to the newly commissioned ensigns and second lieutenants at the NROTC unit at Arizona State University. Admiral Clark began his speech with these words: "Anyone who knows me knows that what I value above all else is investment in people." So, why do we have problems in business?

Let's just take it as a working hypothesis that many of the problems in business management have resulted from the attempt to quantify everything, including human personality characteristics, using big data assessment tools in the employment process. I do not criticize any business for using all the analytical tools at its disposal to select the right applicant for a job, or to ensure that the instinctual, experiential, and/or educational characteristics of an applicant are a good fit for a position being filled. Nor am I dismissive of the need to appraise performance, so long as the appraiser's bias can be minimized or eliminated. But a mind-set focused on scores is a mind-set that looks for numbers to measure performance, and without much difficulty, it becomes a mind-set focused on the numbers themselves. Scoring performance can become the basis for comparison and criticism.

Management is likely less aware of employee motivations, and whether their most important resources—human beings—are having their basic needs fulfilled. Properly understood, the needs of people point to the tools needed for managers to boost performance. Yet, it is not just rank-and-file employees who should be asked what they need. Progressive HR professionals today are suggesting managers be asked what tools they need, as well. I believe that is good advice, but sometimes managers overlook the most obvious tool of all, and it is one that may not be on a list of tools:

good human relations. Managers who understand the truth behind the need for good human relations become good leaders.

> Paul Thomas, entrepreneur in residence at Northern Arizona University, holds that interviewing potential employees for positions is somewhat like dating— you're finding out if they want to be part of this relationship. And if you, the interviewer, have a sincere interest in finding out what this person wants to be, to achieve, to learn, you'll have a good chance of making the best match. He adds that you want to hire great people because in the best of times, it's fun to be around them, and in the worst of times you need their positive attitudes and productivity. "If we are out on a cruise ship and it goes down and you're in a boat with 20 people, do you want them whining and complaining or trying to figure out the best way to stay alive?"

In a time where books on effective business leadership proliferate, I am inviting management to think about those who must follow those leaders, and about how to inspire trust on the part of those who will follow.

In the wilderness where so many cowboys are required to lead herds of cattle up and down narrow canyon trails, there is an old maxim: "If you undertake to lead the herd down the trail, it is best to look back once in a while to see if the herd is following." Animals follow where they have gone before and where they trust the leader. Humans are not all that different.

The best way to earn employee trust is to demonstrate care and concern for the employees' legitimate needs for fulfillment. Our employees, our colleagues, are not automated machines without feelings or ambitions. They desire to share—to give of oneself and contribute to the activities at hand. Sharing is also linked to the needs employees have to express themselves, to be heard. While robotics are taking over some of the mechanical functions previously served by people in their work, robotics are not likely to ever match the creative imagination and the will to share possessed by the human resource.

The best way to demonstrate care and concern for employees is to follow the People-Focused Principles of Management

1. Give people a purpose.
2. Communicate widely.
3. Accommodate/manage change.
4. Create a culture of worth.
5. Create a culture of hope.
6. Reward performance.
7. Create a vision of participation in determining the future of the company.
8. Express gratitude.

These principles are not always followed in practice, and where they are not, the whole enterprise suffers to some degree. Certainly the employees will be unfilled, and thus emotionally unhappy, but the overall productivity and competitiveness of a business will also suffer. Implementing these principles consistently and effectively will boost productivity and profits.

GIVE PEOPLE A PURPOSE

There is only one time that is important—NOW! It is the most important time because it is the only time we have any power over.

—Attributed to Leo Tolstoy

GIVE PEOPLE A purpose, and do it now. Better yet, let them participate in devising the ways and means of accomplishing the mission statement of the organization. This will activate motivation.

There's a classic story about two brick workers, and when asked what they are doing, the first replies that he is laying row after back-breaking row of brick. The second says he is building a beautiful cathedral that will help people glorify God for centuries to come. An aware manager can help employees feel like the second worker.

People want and need to feel their work has meaning. The mission statement of the business must be clear and known to the employees, and it helps greatly if the function of each job in the organization can also be described in terms that make the purpose of each task clear. The employee should be able to see and understand the entire system at work and the role of a given job within the system.

Everyone should know why they come to work—what the business is trying to do in the world—and be able to explain that they go to work for far more than their paycheck. If your employees had to explain what they do in one line—in essence, give an elevator speech—could they do it? Would it be dreary ("I spend my time collating reports of numbers that track widget production"), or would it be stirring ("I spend my time helping people around the world feel safe in their homes and offices because they use our widgets")?

It is critical that one's work feels like a contribution, giving the sense of purpose, which is one of the reasons this principle, "Give People a Purpose," is stressed here with a sense of urgency, especially where there are workers without a sense of purpose. The reason this principle is so important is that it is related to three of the basic human needs for fulfillment: the need to belong; the need to matter (to have meaning); and the need to share (to contribute, to give of oneself). Senior business executives have told me they recognize their business needs to manage millennials differently than people have been managed in the past since they seem to value making a difference more than making money. The truth is, everyone needs to feel that he or she has made a difference, somehow, somewhere. Millennials are a valuable and powerful work force; forward-thinking companies will actively seek to recruit millennials by helping them see how they can make a difference by working for their company.

We know a sense of purpose is present when people are motivated by the mission of the organization and brainstorm ideas to try to help with the mission's successful outcome. Purpose is also present when people can describe their own efforts in relationship to the purpose of the organization.

Remaining focused on the purpose of an enterprise for the moment, one has to envy the clearheaded purpose kept in mind by the American farmer. Farmers have been justifiably proud for many years of their connection to the function of feeding people. Their identification with that purpose is even more easily obtained when the focus is on feeding the part of the world that is in extreme poverty. In fact, the productivity and efficiency of the American farmer is enviable, for it is the surplus product produced by American farmers that produces a positive balance of payments for the American economy and goes a long way toward meeting the rest of the world's needs for food and fiber. Of course, American farmers will never feed the world by themselves, but they consistently produce in excess of the needs of American consumers, and the excess is available for export. Many people around the world clearly need that excess production. For purposes of this text, the point is: clarity of purpose has helped motivate efficiencies and productivity in American agriculture.

People who work in healthcare also have the opportunity to enjoy a clear purpose and function in the products and services they provide, because everyone values good health.

Other examples of work having a purpose include work that contributes to safety of food, industrial equipment, workplaces, chemicals in common use, toys, and automobiles. These examples are highly motivating because of the desirable outcome—safety being the priority. The same could be said for work in education and work to remediate environmental disasters. But, all work is useful to someone, and people need to feel they are making a contribution. It is important that the purpose of their work be clear.

Admittedly, it is easier to identify the purpose of work when one is focused on the mission statement of the organization and harder to do so when one must connect the function of each job to the overall mission statement. When each worker can clearly see how his or her efforts contribute to the overall accomplishment of the mission statement, some degree of job satisfaction can be safely assumed.

For decades now, managers have been taught to use some degree of systems thinking when organizing work and industrial processes. It is a small thing to ask these same managers to additionally explain, illustrate, and emphasize how each person's work contributes to the overall system that is operative in a workplace, both in terms of how the system supports the individual worker and how the worker supports the system. In fact, it will be healthy for the manager to connect his/her people to the system's functions in a very personal way. Otherwise, it is too easy to fall into managing functions instead of people.

Too often, the reliance on business metrics translates the purpose of work into nothing more than financial yield for the employer. Though profits in the business world or net revenues in the nonprofit world are very important, work is much nobler than financial yield. Lasting motivation also requires a reminder of why we do work in the first place.

To illustrate purpose-driven work over metrics, I share the following anecdote:

> A young woman worked as a development officer for one of the Arizona universities. As such, she understood herself as being in the relationship business— building constructive relationships between the university and its graduates. She cared as much for the donors as individuals as she did about their potential

giving to the university. Like the young woman I am describing, her immediate manager was heartbroken one day when she found out that one of her largest donors, a lovely lady she had come to know and dream with over more than five years, had passed away. The young employee knew that her boss had come to understand this woman as a friend and kindred spirit in the vision of offering higher education and better prospects for students. Understandably, then, the boss was shocked, appalled, and insulted to hear that their director's response to the woman's passing was: "Oh good! So that will activate the giving from the estate plan!" For reasons and responses like this, the young woman's boss resigned very soon after this event. The young woman was not long in following. Work has to be about more than the metrics and financial yield. It has to be about purpose, and living/working into that purpose should be based on relationships.

Today, the conscious capitalism movement is helping businesses remember that over and above all the work that is done in pursuit of profits, there is a public function to be served. I recall learning in law school about the development and early history of the corporation in England, when the king issued charters to those selected to meet a public need through the business receiving the charter. The whole point was to help the king meet public need, though today we more often refer to public demand. Interestingly, lawyers today are still taught that when a corporation is formed today through the filing of articles of incorporation, the approval of that document by the corporation commission or other regulatory agency becomes a charter. Articles of incorporation themselves are often referred to as the corporate charter. The point here is not about terms or nomenclature. The point is to recall that the very existence of the business depends upon a social contract between the entrepreneur and the public at large—a public service is to be rendered. Meeting a public need is the rationale for the enterprise. Enlightened business leaders think in those terms and are often justifiably proud of the service they provide. The same can be said for those who are at the helm of nonprofit corporations. Whisper n Thunder is an inspiring example of a nonprofit corporation served by volunteer directors and a volunteer president who serve because of their passion for a public purpose (charitable). Among other things, this group makes heating oil available in winter to native people living in remote locations on Native American reservations; it provides encouragement and leadership training for young native women; and it has an online thought journal that has millions of hits on the internet. The development of this organization is an inspiring story worth reading. An excursus into its website and online thought journal is well worth the effort.

Another example of giving employees a purpose involves a company called SEMCO, also written about in "Firms of Endearment: How World Class Companies Profit from Passion and Purpose." Ricardo Semler took over SEMCO from his father, but then had a heart attack. In response to this health crisis, rather than just change his life, he changed the company as well. He asked employees to suggest their own pay levels, review their bosses' performances, and learn to do one another's jobs. He eliminated a central office, opened the books to all employees, and set up a profit-sharing plan. He made all meetings voluntary and vacation time compulsory.

Talk about giving employees a sense of purpose! It sounds as though these actions could be the plan for "How to Go Bankrupt in a Year." But purposeful employees increased the company's sales from $35 million to $212 million in six years, grew from several hundred employees to three thousand, and the annual turnover rate plummeted to 1 percent!

The story about SEMCO is a part of the evidence from case studies proving the importance of people having a purpose. Now I must acknowledge that people can have an individual purpose in life that is unrelated to their purpose at work. Though the two are related and there is overlap, I am focused on the latter context. If the object is to activate human capital at work, people must have a purpose at work and understand it, own it. In fact, countless studies have demonstrated that of the most significant factors in employee motivation, commitment, and job satisfaction one of them is simply this—what is expected of the employee is clear to the employee.

Regarding the idea that passion is necessary but can't be taught: okay, but passion can be cultivated.

Having said that, there appear to be two kinds of passion. One is more or less tied to the instincts and inclinations we have. The other is born out of life experience, where we find that the work we are doing is recognized, appreciated, and promoted. In this context we feel that we have found a place that will support the fulfillment of our human goals as well as our basic needs in providing security for ourselves and our families. It seems possible to achieve personal goals. In that place, we are likely to feel that we have found a workplace that honors who we truly are as people. This kind of passion can be cultivated because we are helping people find a home, and when it feels like a match, people will be passionate about the match.

The public service component of business purpose gets lost in the lives of some employees. Why? First, annual reporting requires attention to metrics that are not purpose-based in terms of their focus; we need some new or additional metrics that consider purpose and support purpose—for example, "On a scale of one to ten, how knowledgeable are you of the extent to which your individual work contributes to the company's purpose?" Or "How well do you believe your company is meeting a public need?" Second, specialization of jobs requires skills so technical they can seem separate from the purpose of the organization—but they never should be. How can a passion be developed for employees in these situations?

> A highly successful workplace written about in "Firms of Endearment" is SAS Institute, a developer of analytic software. It boasts thirty-seven consecutive years of record revenues and earnings and employs thirteen thousand people worldwide. Only 2 percent voluntarily leave in a given year, compared to 22 percent industry-wide. Last year it had sixty-five thousand applicants for 433 positions. Its four stated and well-known principles are: Value people as much as possible; to give is to get; trust above all things; ensure that employees understand the significance of their work. Those can't be merely words on a website; they have to be backed up by management living out each of the four principles. As the SAS Institute example clearly illustrates, when such words are followed by action, profits soar.

Each of you reading this book can and should reflect on what this principle means to you. Here are some examples of what might come to mind:

DISCUSSION QUESTIONS

1. Let us suppose you are doing a job that is being done adequately by someone else, as well. If you feel you are doing your job well but the other person thinks the whole thing is kind of

dumb, but it produces a paycheck, is there a problem? Or put the shoes on the other person's feet. The other person does the job well, but you think the whole thing is kind of dumb (yet it is a paycheck). Is it a problem now?

2. Does public recognition of the service being provided where you work help motivate you to do better or work harder? Has that public recognition become an asset to your company or enterprise? Reflecting on these things, does your purpose at work become an asset to the company? (I think so.)

3. To what extent does your purpose at work depend upon being in right relationship with things and people? To what extent does this question properly extend beyond the context of your workplace and into the public square (so to speak)?

4. To what extent are you offended if your boss misunderstands your need for "right relationships" with others in the organization, starting with the boss?

5. If your grandson or granddaughter comes to you in twenty years and says he or she is not sure it will be possible to make a difference in the world, what will you say?

Here are some words to work by: "What are we trying to accomplish?" Every staff meeting, memo, and communication should remind people of their collective purpose and offer one reflection of something done that gets closer to accomplishing it.

Giving people a purpose will help activate human capital.

COMMUNICATE WIDELY

Leaders who make it a practice to draw out the thoughts and ideas of their subordinates and who are receptive even to bad news will be properly informed. Communicate downward to subordinates with at least the same care and attention as you communicate upward to superiors.

—L. B. Belker

The basic building block of good communication is the feeling that every human being is unique and of value.

—Unknown

TOO MANY PEOPLE today work in information silos. Information silos should not be tolerated; instead, business managers should communicate widely. Systems analysis is an important management tool, and an auxiliary benefit from using systems thinking is that it can enable managers to orient their employees to the larger context of their work. A sense of purpose can be developed when employees can clearly see how their work contributes to the smooth functioning of the entire system that is the context for their work. Obviously, the basic parts of the system, and the contributions of each part, must be effectively communicated in order for the purpose of the whole to be clear. Communication and information combine to enhance the appreciation of the system. Communication is not just about helping people see and understand a purpose for their work. When silos are broken down, it becomes easier for managers and indeed teams of workers to seek ideas, promote imagination, and increase the effectiveness of each employee.

> One business, BW Papersystems, facing drastic times asked employees for cost-saving ideas, and implemented $20 million worth of them, which combined with other measures avoided layoffs—and served the company well on a continuing basis. Had the company considered only those ideas coming from the top tier of management, that success would not have been achieved.

Sometimes managers promote the use of open space work environments to foster improved communication. I have seen creative work environments, almost like a Starbucks, where people could carry their laptops anywhere in a huge open space, talk across long tables, and creative communication seemed greatly enhanced. Open space work environments may not be the best way to foster communication while maintaining high levels of worker efficiency and productivity, but widespread, almost instantaneous communication has many virtues, including some increased efficiency in the longer term.

A transportation planner with a graduate degree in planning worked in a regional agency where reports were prepared without people being told why the information was requested or how it would be used. The planner worked inside a transportation agency that concerns itself with levels of traffic on public roadways and plans for infrastructure expansion when necessary. It had divided itself, as many agencies do, into departments. She told us that when she walked over to request data from the modeling department, the staff there didn't know the data they were producing was being used in a major study to add lanes to a freeway, and even worse, really didn't know, or hadn't thought about the fact that the data they were producing was supposed to emulate conditions they experienced while commuting to work every day! She was disappointed to learn that her colleagues had been left out of contextual conversations that might clue them in on why their work was important. She was even more disappointed to learn that she was the first one to explain why she was requesting the data in the first place. Needless to say, in a situation like that, an individual has no sense of connection with the overall planning process. Even this planner found that the overall planning perspective (big picture) she gained through her completion of a graduate degree was frequently underutilized. All of the education the planner received was a resource just looking for an application. Partly because of the existence of information silos, this planner felt underutilized. Indeed, it was not just a feeling. The fact is she was underutilized. The administrative or management practice that left this planner in an information silo was highly demotivating. She no longer works for that agency.

In another example, one of the most lauded businesses in terms of a successful people-focused management style is the Container Store, which shares all financial data with employees to give them a true sense of both productivity and what challenges are being met.

Also, the CEO of a famous charitable organization discovered that the annual reports, which outline successes, were not being distributed internally. Annual reports are not only figures that stockholders and others use to assess success; they have become powerful marketing tools that can and should be shared with internal audiences as well. By changing the procedure and making sure each employee received the colorful brochure with uplifting stories of the results of their organization, the CEO created a significant lift in morale at all staffing levels.

Managers sometimes fail to anticipate how many good ideas will come back to them if they communicate their own challenges, or even the routine requirements facing them each day. Admittedly, a manager can ask employees for suggestions on how a unit can do things more effectively and not receive any replies. I have gone through this experience. However, if that same manager has created a team climate in which imagination, open communication, initiative, and ambition are all encouraged, a strong sense of mutual commitment creates synergy, and from time to time an employee will share an idea that can be transformative to the productivity of that team. A positive experience will encourage even more ideas. Time and again, employees have come alive with excitement when they realize their ideas are valued. This is, of course, related to the basic human need for fulfillment addressed in this chapter: the need to express or be heard. People seek an opportunity to demonstrate their uniqueness. They want to demonstrate their authentic selves where possible. They want to be understood. The coming alive will never happen if there aren't meaningful opportunities for open, meaningful, and safe communication between employee and supervisor.

> Gail Bradley has worked at Northern Trust in a variety of positions for decades and possesses a strong institutional memory. She is presently a Vice-President in the Wealth Strategies Group. She recalls a senior manager faced with a morale problem in the institution.
>
> "He was not a warm fuzzy guy; he was a quantitative guy with a Harvard, MBA. But he was willing to step out of his comfort zone, an admirable trait in a senior manager. He put fifteen of the biggest complainers on a committee and asked them to suggest solutions. Then he listened, and began having brown bag lunches with a few employees at a time. He made himself available and was willing to answer any questions posed to him in this comfortable setting."
>
> Also at his direction, his department managers' quarterly reports, minus any personal information, were posted online, affording transparent communication of status and success for his employees. No wonder Northern Trust enjoys a stellar reputation. Open communication, the mutual and valued sharing of ideas and information, and the key skill of listening works very well.

Even employees with little ambition or imagination will feel the need to know about the overall direction of their company because they need to feel they belong. Frequent memos, group briefings, and shared financial reports (such as those being prepared for routine distribution to investors or regulatory agencies) all contribute to the employees' sense that *they matter*. All employees of an enterprise deserve to have at least as much information about their company as is distributed to the general public. Too often this is not the case unless the employees conduct their own research. That shouldn't be necessary.

Internal communications are often restricted to those who are deemed to have a need to know. It will do no harm, however, to rephrase the question of who needs to know, to include those who will potentially benefit from being included in the communication. It's incredible how much information is published and disclosed, and public documents are filled with information that employees should know or at the very least would probably like to know. This merely requires awareness on the part of management of the benefits of sharing that information internally and with intention.

It should go without saying that one of the most demotivating experiences an employee can have is being altogether overlooked with respect to a hastily called meeting where the person who was forgotten absolutely should be there and justifiably would expect to be there. This can be demoralizing at the very least. I had the personal experience of being overlooked in this way and know firsthand how bad it feels. Hurried communications, including hastily called meetings, are potentially fraught with unanticipated consequences.

On this point, inertia can be a powerful force. Sometimes it's easy to consistently "forget" to include an employee who tends to slow things down with too many examples or irrelevant observations. If this situation exists, it can serve as a wake-up call to a supervisor to see rather than ignore a potential problem, an opportunity exists to first help a troublesome employee become more productive, and if remedial methods are ineffective, to consider reassignment.

Communication should also be evaluated with reference to being reasonably comprehensive. Lots of e-mail today is almost indecipherable either because of shortcuts in the use of language or the time pressures under which the e-mail is created in the first place. Hurried responses sometimes make for inadequate communication. While queries are often longer and more carefully crafted than responses, responses can be so inadequate that there is ample room for misinterpretation of the response. Each workplace should develop its own e-mail protocols. The most extreme example of brief communication comes from a former executive at Intel who said everyone in his organization knew they were not to send him an e-mail unless it could be answered in a single word: yes or no. While there may be some humor in this example, it proves the observation that a query may have to be much more extensive and carefully crafted than the response. Most business communications should not be so abbreviated; people need meaningful guidance and want to understand the basis upon which decisions are made, and most businesses are not as professionally and extensively staffed as Intel. Furthermore, most communications are not to the CEO. Most communications are among team members or between a team and its first-level manager.

Why does communication suffer, really? Communication takes time—understanding takes more—and we consistently hear "no one has enough time." Also, project deadlines are often specific to a team and project, making it easy to become insular in thinking. Efficient e-mail management is a must in today's employee tool box, but the content of communications must be enough to serve the intended purpose of the message.

The reference to e-mail also illustrates another common problem in business today; people are talking less to each other. Reliance on e-mails, texting, and social media has prompted people to communicate quickly. At some point there must be real conversation between any two or more people who expect an understanding of the context of a communication. Even Twitter feeds, originally limited to 140 characters, have identified my propensity for brief communication. Yet a January 5, 2016, announcement in the *Wall Street Journal* said the company announced its plan to extend its 140-character limit to as many as ten thousand characters. This was met with some pushback, with some preferring the "brevity and speed of the real-time service."

Good managers know communicating widely and meeting with employees regularly is critical. While it is impractical for the CEO to schedule meetings with all employees, middle management can serve as a conduit for information. The direct supervisor should be aware of an employee's challenges and situation. If each manager can have a meeting, even if a brief one, with every employee who reports to him or her, the benefits can be incalculable: people can ask questions instead of running to other employees trying to get information; they see and are buoyed by their manager's interest, and sometimes surprising things may come out of such a meeting.

> Pete Wilson, of Mesa, Arizona, worked for Control Data for twelve years, and he had thirty-five hundred people reporting to him. Control Data promoted laterally, moving people into other areas of the company to learn something new. That required training, of course, and people had questions. Pete was required to talk to each employee at least quarterly, sometimes individually and sometimes in small groups—the important thing was that employees got to ask questions. Pete managed by wandering around. He was there with his employees all the time. Pete said: "The company put

a lot of effort into manager training at all levels, but what was even more powerful was communication. It was two times as valuable as training because it led to trust." Pete added that his own manager's trust of him meant leaving him alone, which motivated Pete even more to work productively and well as an individual and a leader.

In conversation, one can test whether any assumption is shared, whether the same facts are known, whether a common objective is in mind. Technology has made communication more efficient but can ironically have a damaging effect on communication and relationships. When it becomes an excuse for not actually speaking to people, it almost certainly will be demeaning. In actuality, many employees don't understand why others in the company don't call them on the phone.

A successful advertising agency, The Lavidge Company, has survived when many have folded by making sure employees feel included. Photographs of all staff members are prominently displayed in the lobby, illustrating that the CEO is not the only face of the firm. While some employees may not care about that, it is likely many do. Moreover, this practice sends a message to the public regarding the emphasis placed on the importance of all staff, and it communicates to employees that the company knows who they are. It is a different form of communication than we have been discussing, but it is communication nonetheless.

Communication doesn't have to be two-way to dramatically affect employees. An executive in residence at NAU, Paul Thomas, found out that a CEO sent everyone a holiday card. He decided to go one step above and send each employee a birthday card with a handwritten line and signature. Those cards sprouted up on cubicle walls throughout the workplace. People felt they mattered.

At this point, another moment of reflection might be in order.

DISCUSSION QUESTIONS

1. Is it fundamentally wrong when people don't know how their work is used?
2. Who has been the best communicator you have ever observed or with whom you have communicated?
3. Who has been the worst?
4. What stood out in those persons' attitude and behavior?
5. If the transportation planner mentioned at the beginning of this chapter had told you her story, what would you have liked to say to her manager?
6. When have you been the most and least motivated in your life?
7. If your grandson/granddaughter comes to you in twenty years and tells you that his/her manager has never spoken to him/her directly, what would you say?

The importance of frequent, timely, and focused communication on improving employee performance cannot be overemphasized. Once again I am describing a management principle that contributes to activating human capital. Perhaps it should be an intentional daily practice to initiate communication with others in your workplace.

5

ACCOMMODATE/MANAGE CHANGE

Culture does not change because we desire to change it. Culture changes when the organization is transformed; the culture reflects the realities of people working together every day.

—Frances Hesselbein

ADAPTABILITY CAN BE an important factor in the productivity and effectiveness of both managers and people who are managed. The ability to accommodate and manage change also contributes to the sustainability of an enterprise. A recent lecture at a Human Capital Institute forum on managing talent emphasized the point. The speaker was associated with Doctors Without Borders, an organization that enjoys the benefit of managing people who have a high level of passion for their work. It is also an organization that has necessarily promoted the principle of accommodating and managing change aggressively. Doctors in the field with minimal support, and often in circumstances marred by war, natural disasters, or disease, know the situation they will face tomorrow will be quite different than the one they face today. While those conditions are usually more challenging than ones faced in most businesses today, the pace of modern business often requires faster management responses than traditional management models have assumed. At the same forum, one speaker said his company altogether abandoned the concept of an annual performance review. In being able to respond quickly to changing market conditions, his company has weekly sessions in which performance is evaluated and adjustments are made in work assignments. That practice anticipates change and manages it effectively. On the other hand, the purpose of meeting frequently must be clearly understood. Otherwise, employees may feel the manager doesn't trust them and the manager is looking for the employees to justify their performance for that week. Frequent meetings may be interpreted as micromanaging, but not if it is about timely reactions to external and internal changes impacting the company.

While not always practical, frequent performance reviews reveal evolving expectations—a change employees need to know and understand. An annual performance review does not give employees feedback about performance with sufficient frequency. Managers have choices, and more frequent evaluations may serve the interests of all concerned. Personal interviews in between performance evaluations may be even more valuable. The conversation will be more focused, and this action will signal a care and concern for the welfare of the employee. The employee can also take advantage of a personal conversation to make requests in terms of what might be helpful: opportunity to attend a special course or training, authorization to shadow a role model, or the assignment of a formal mentor. In any case, personal interviews increase personal attention compared to an annual written report submitted to the employee, where the only real reaction by the employee may be to sign or refuse to do so. Written reports without verbal reviews often stifle conversation, and an impersonal form of communication is even considered to be demeaning by many people. To restate, the verbal performance review is generally far superior to the more formalized written process.

> To me, more important than the six years of written reports I received during active military duty was the day I was leaving Cuba to take another assignment. My commanding officer wanted me to know he thought the new assignment was a mistake. Without knowing the background behind my choice, he urged me to seek assignment in another fleet squadron, saying the assignment offered would be a waste of potential, because, "You have flag rank in you." (He meant, "You have the potential to become an admiral.") That had never been in any written report, but being said in person made a significant impression. The impact was enormous because it was surprising and flattering. The commanding officer could have said, "I would like to see you promoted as soon as possible." But he didn't. Unexpected praise issued directly is powerful.

In fast-paced businesses where feedback is almost constant, whether it's sharing glory or pointing out where someone missed the mark, the frequency of course correction in real time, as opposed to long after the fact, is far preferable- so much so it could supersede the impact of any routine performance review in value to the business. The old adage of praise in public and criticize in private continues to be applicable as a constraint on feedback issued too hastily and without consideration of the immediate circumstances or context in which the communication is taking place.

Businesses need to be prepared to manage change when employees are incentivized and/or rewarded for new ideas that get implemented, people volunteer ideas at staff meetings, and managers make time to consult their staff. The change prompted through these processes is desirable, but it is still change, which may bring unanticipated consequences. In any event, businesses will want to manage change for maximum beneficial results.

Managers should proactively signal to everyone in the organization that management values change—not change for change's sake, but change when it energizes people, increases productivity, promotes efficiency, and creates a competitive advantage in the marketplace.

In addition, the source of the idea associated with change can be top down, bottom up, or even from outside the organization. It doesn't matter where the ideas come from; the important thing is that the organization be sufficiently aware and open to good ideas and then react to good ideas when they surface. Grass roots and grass tops all have something to offer.

Many consultants offer courses in change management, particularly when new IT systems are deployed or there are other major changes imposed on the workplace, which require either technical training or the adaptation of new standard operating policies and procedures. Managing such change is appropriate and necessary, but this is not the sort of change referenced here.

The change I seek is the change that originates with creative, imaginative, and motivated employees. Such employees may initiate or at least suggest new ways of pursuing the company mission, ways that could increase efficiency and profitability. Setting the stage for that kind of change requires both of the preceding principles to be actively pursued: identifying purpose and communicating widely. When those principles are followed, managers can reasonably expect more ambitious subordinates to work with greater clarity and motivation, resulting in the energy that managers expect their employees to bring to work every day.

It's been said the six most dangerous words in today's world are "We've always done it this way." When managers indicate they are open and accommodating to new ideas they are elevating the possibility of significant success—and as a bonus, their employees are excited about that prospect.

> Let's look at a case that involved a Hayssen worker who had been working overseas at a foreign plant, and returned to a position in the United States. After some weeks passed, he gave his resignation. When the supervisor asked about his reasons for resigning, the worker addressed his concerns about his value to the company. He said that while he'd been away, he'd felt trusted; no one made him punch a time clock; he was able to move from one area to another without a key card; and he felt like he was a valuable addition to the team. Coming back to the more restrictive domestic environment helped him realize the type of workplace he wanted. Fortunately, his manager saw value in these comments and was able to prevail in seeking appropriate policy changes so the US factories reflected the same practices.

> Commerce Bank is known for instituting a practice now widely used, which is "kill a stupid rule." Anyone can find and point out such a rule and in many businesses even receive a reward for doing so. Such a policy both accommodates and manages change.

What some managers fail to see is the responsibility they have for activating employee energy and giving it license to work in support of the company.

> My business manager, Tracie, had worked for me for a couple months, and I thought we were getting along pretty well, but I noticed that she would apologize several times a day. She would begin sentences with. "I'm sorry if you've already thought about this ..." or "This might not be the right time for me to mention that ..." One day we had finished a meeting for which Tracie had done all the research and preparation, so it was natural that as the meeting went on she took the lead, posing questions and running an interview, and I mostly took notes. After we were finished, to my utter surprise, Tracie apologized for taking over and running the meeting! I told her, "You must have had some really insecure bosses in the past—you did a great job!" She told me that in the past if she was perceived as learning things too fast or as taking too much initiative, people would tell her to slow down because she looked like she was trying to get the boss's job. Unleashing employee energy as a way of encouraging constructive change must be done without penalty for the demonstration of ambition, creativity, and leadership.

In workplaces where people are ignored or the mangers signal they don't want to be bothered, most workers will put in their time, resign themselves to being unhappy at work, and tell their friends and family members, "That's why they call it work." By contrast, where employees can look forward to having their ideas valued, they are much more likely to bring a positive attitude to work. I remember an occasion about twenty years ago when leading executives in Silicon Valley industries explained the success of their companies: "We encourage employees to fail." Those companies valued experimentation, creativity, and change. And it is change that became a necessary business assumption—the businesses would neither have existed nor thrived without the ability to create new products and processes. In workplaces that embrace experimentation, creativity, and change, people consider their employment to be more like play than work. Anyone who has watched children learn through experimentation can well imagine the same sort of process can work for adults as well. Google has encouraged its employees to take time away from work in order to imagine new processes. Not everyone is prepared to deploy their workers in this way, but change can nevertheless be promoted, especially when it contributes to a competitive position in the marketplace.

The dynamic in Silicon Valley is associated with a culture that values innovation, but for purposes of this book, the value here is not innovation, per se. It is a management attitude that is prepared to accommodate innovation or other change and manage that change effectively. In fact, one of the basic human needs for fulfillment is the need for change. People have an ability to create, and they want to explore possibilities, to experience variety. Employees can be expected to embrace some change—if it is carefully explained and implemented.

The willingness to manage change will be reduced if the change is perceived as a threat to the status quo and desired predictability, invites criticism, or if the change seems to require too much effort.

> When faced with employees voting to unionize, Whole Foods CEO John Mackey visited all 145 stores and listened to his employees nationwide. Addressing their

concerns, he ended up not only completely covering health insurance but issuing debit cards to spend on medical and dental costs. Employees decertified unions.

Mr. Mackey's response to a perceived threat was immediate and dynamic, but it was also reactive. Other persons advocate planning in advance to cope with the effects of evolving change. In fact, some people start movements to promote such planning.

Kimber Lanning is an energetic young leader with a strong entrepreneurial bent. She started Local First Arizona, a movement promoting procurement from locally owned businesses. She believes managers who do not embrace change resist it at their own peril.

"The dinosaurs will die out, but we should hasten that. Best practices are hardly done at all, and when you see the CEO salaries over the last twenty years and the discrepancy between that figure and the average working person's salary, it's horrifying."

Furthermore, she believes that companies that do not voluntarily adapt to people-focused management should be dealt with harshly by the consumer.

"All we would need to run these poor practitioners out of business would be to refuse to buy their merchandise. GE has invested billions in India, funded a program to crush unions, then brought back the manufacture of hot water heaters to the United States while paying workers here half what they did before. We could, and perhaps should, stop buying their products until their practices change."

Ms. Lanning's comments above reflect another reality in today's world. Millennials have expectations that defy the traditional approach to economic decision-making. Millennials will readily quit one job in favor of another if they don't like the purposes being pursued by their employers. They are also prone to shifting their buying patterns away from companies with employment practices that are not in alignment with their value systems founded in meaningful impact and purpose.

Millennials are a product of their time as much as the Greatest Generation or Baby Boomers. Recently, students at Northern Arizona University peacefully protested the NAU Foundation's decision to invest in companies the students felt were irresponsible in contributing to causes of climate change, much like how some of us may recall students protesting war. Protesting regarding investment processes based on principles reflects this generation's desire for purpose and impact at community, national, and global levels.

Each generation's values are shaped by current events and innovations in the world; none has a monopoly on greatness or failure. Understanding as much as you can about every employee—which includes the values of their respective generations—makes it easier to bring out the best in each employee.

What is exciting to you about a new idea or approach? Why do you think others don't get excited? Why do you think some people are actually afraid of a new idea? Was there anyone who ever encouraged you to be a trailblazer? Who did you admire who managed change and innovation especially well?

DISCUSSION QUESTIONS

1. If your grandchild comes to you in twenty years and tells you that he or she has been told to just work and not think—and not to try to change anything—what would you say to him or her?

2.　What would you say to the manager involved?

Properly done, accommodating and managing change helps activate human capital. Can we imagine a daily routine that includes the question: What could be changed here?

6

CREATE A CULTURE OF WORTH

There are two things people want more than sex and money ... recognition and praise.

—Mary Kay Ash

THE VALUE IN seeing potential in people and helping people see it in themselves is immeasurable. Creating a culture of worth among employees signals a clear message—management values its people.

One of the basic human needs for fulfillment is personal growth. People want to become more than they are. People want to progress toward their goals too, at least if they still have hope. While employees may have a healthy self-image, activating their growth and moving them toward the fulfillment of their potential requires employers to create a culture of worth in the workplace.

Most of us have grown up in a culture that values the life and potential of each child. Yet, somehow it often happens the potential represented by each life becomes undervalued, at least by those outside the family. Business shares some responsibility in helping each person develop on a wide spectrum appropriate to the business. Talent, knowledge, work experience, and potential contributions should be considered. Knowing how to bring each employee into a smoothly functioning system in the best possible way benefits the entire company.

Personal goals are often undervalued by businesses and in particular, by management. Focus in business is too often limited. It's a matter of "Do you know how to do what I need done right now?" While it may not be stated, the message is "I don't care about the rest of your life; just do your work." Management would benefit from being open to other ways employees could enrich and contribute to the company.

An interviewer of a job applicant could look beyond the boundaries of a job description to see how an individual's gifts and talents can be fully utilized to integrate a potential employee into the existing system. This analysis can also be utilized in performance reviews. That sometimes involves altering the employer's thinking so much that it results in rewriting a job description. A good manager notices when a potential or current employee can reach far beyond the initial or current position, and the manager can benefit greatly by creating a new position or enhancing the current position that will both utilize all of a person's talents and serve the company's objectives.

Both employers and employees should be dedicated to improving the human condition in the workplace as well as outside of it. There might be all kinds of reasons given for this commitment, some even philosophical. But, the most compelling reason comes from innovative business leaders who are convinced that a business failing to create a culture of worth will be economically irrelevant within a few years. The prediction is socially conscious consumers will simply take their business elsewhere. Some businesses may not have to be concerned with this prospect—but for those that ultimately rely on consumers, the forewarning has been given.

Too many businesses operate with the basic attitude that it is necessary to reduce the personnel expense in their companies before looking at other possibilities for reducing costs. Apart from the expense of personnel, one often hears from business leaders that the other compelling reason for replacing people with automated processes is that most challenges of management are with people and their problems. However, this disregards the fact people in management are also people and could very well be the root of the problem more so than the personnel. While one should not underestimate the amount of time needed to effectively manage people, certainly technical and mechanical processes have problems of their own. Whatever the virtue of automation, machines will not generate the new ideas needed to create new product lines, achieve a competitive position in the marketplace, identify new markets altogether, and lead companies to a new future (as opposed to declining in a typical business cycle). Current business news is replete with reports that the business cycle is accelerating (shortening) for many businesses today. Does this mean businesses are failing? Failure to utilize human resources to the maximum degree possible may be somewhat responsible for shortening the business cycle. *People must be valued as a fundamental business asset.* Is it not a violation of business ethics for managers to disparage their "business assets" (employees) by assuming employees are the expendable resource. Is it not wrong to assume employees are always grousing, looking for a way to slack off, stealing property from company inventories, or doing something else more negative than positive while on the job?

The book *Firms of Endearment* noted that in a study of twenty-eight companies that invest in their employees in ways similar to our People-Focused Principles of Management, eighteen of which are publicly traded, the return on investment for them was more than 1,000 percent, compared to an average of 122 percent for companies that don't follow these practices—an eight-to-one ratio. Those companies include Costco, FedEx, Google, Harley-Davidson, Southwest Airlines, United Parcel Service, Starbucks, Disney, Whole Foods Market, Nordstrom, and MasterCard.

Valued employees can become a point of pride to the company and often to the communities where the company does business. It is not by accident that elected officials court the finest companies, chambers of commerce recognize corporate citizenship, and the average citizen points with pride to the existence of employment opportunities in their locale. The contributions to civic life that a company touts as giving back to a community are often the result of volunteer efforts by employees who are inspired to action by properly oriented company leadership. The goodwill generated by those employees creates great worth with minimal cost to the company; it is a worth that extends far beyond near-term profitability, especially when employees are motivated on a continuing basis through management's adoption of the principles in this book.

A creative mind is one of the most underutilized assets in today's workplace. Businesses are so focused on the directives to "assemble more widgets" or "crunch more numbers" that they aren't entertaining thoughts like "What might work better?" and "How else could this be done?" Companies that encourage employees to think creatively could pull far ahead of the competition in revenue and employee retention. No two minds work alike; if you give your employees encouragement to think about the business process where they work, you might be amazed at what they give you in return.

> Perhaps one of the most radical examples of creating a culture of worth can be found at Zappos, an online shoe and clothing store. The CEO of Zappos, John Hsieh, announced that as of 4/30/15, "In order to eliminate the legacy management hierarchy, there will be effectively no more people managers." Imagine the reaction of people who realized they could work in a whole new way because the company wished to relate to people differently than before.
>
> In an interview with Salt River Project ("SRP") General Manager Mark Bonsall, I asked how SRP develops its people. Mark leaned back and said with a big smile, "Well, first of all, we have great people here."

I've been running around saying many executives I know think employees are a problem. They'd just like to get rid of them—automate if possible—because people are expensive, bring problems to work, and sometimes don't even come to work. Contrast that attitude with Mark Bonsall's attitude when he said SRP has great people. I know SRP inside and out, and he's right, SRP does have great people. Part of their success is the culture in which they're working. Yet even though SRP has great people, I know something else about these people; they're expensive, they bring their problems to work, sometimes they don't come to work, and many of their functions could be automated. But when your CEO sees you as one of his great assets, you become as great as you can be.

As importantly, an individual's sense of worth also depends in

large measure upon whether a supervisor can offer a human response to a very human situation. There are times when people
need a little time-out from the usual expectations because of life
circumstances. They would hope to be treated as people of worth,
deserving of consideration. Here's an example of how not to do it.

> A young couple was expecting their first child and was
> trying to get everything worked out with their respec-
> tive employers for maternity and paternity leave. In
> fact, the husband had asked the HR department at
> his company about paternity leave policies before he
> accepted employment there and was told it was avail-
> able. So when the time came the husband talked to
> his manager, requesting four weeks of paternity leave.
> "Four weeks!" the manager said. "Why?" The husband
> looked at him and said, "Because it's my first baby and
> my wife is going to need some help." His manager
> looked back at him and said, "Oh—well when my kid
> was born I didn't take any time off, so I just assumed
> you wouldn't either." Sadly this story gets a little worse.
> When the husband went back to HR about his pater-
> nity leave request, they informed him, "Well, we're go-
> ing to need a doctor's note verifying that your wife
> will need your help." The doctor was only too willing
> to provide one and also asked if he needed a prescrip-
> tion for a new workplace! The husband felt demeaned
> and couldn't avoid the conclusion that his personal life
> circumstances didn't matter to his manager.

In short, I know that in some places there is a culture of worth
where management encourages use of earned personal and sick
time to take care of personal matters. Why does this not happen
everywhere? I have a suspicion that in too many places, compassion
is interpreted as a sign of weakness. Excessive time off is interpreted

as indifference to workplace needs, but what is considered excessive varies widely among employers.

Contrast the attitudes of the husband's manager with the attitude of a manager who sends a quick e-mail to support employees when they are absent for reasons that are personal yet compelling to them.

Sometimes managers do understand their employees need to feel worthy. At work you earn this feeling of worthiness by going above and beyond, and some managers are determined to force people to earn it. But, this should not be an opportunity to take advantage of an employee. Examples of taking advantage could include asking for and getting commitments for unpaid overtime and expecting executives or professional staff to routinely come in on weekends to work. Even salaried employees begin to resent that. It could also translate to manipulation of people, giving them more and more work because you've got a certain number of proven performers. Using the maxim that if you need something done you should give it to a busy person, you'd rather rely on that person rather than allocate the work to someone with the time to get it done. Management may choose to avoid taking the time to teach, instruct, mentor, or monitor someone not as experienced, taking advantage of those already apt at "getting things done."

In every workplace there are times when unpaid overtime, weekend work by salaried people, and more work given to employees with full portfolios become realities that come up from time to time, and no one should be angered by an occasional instance. On the other hand, it is of great concern when these practices and expectations are routine in the workplace.

This may seem counterintuitive, but research from Stanford University shows that productivity per hour declines sharply when the workplace exceeds fifty hours, and drops off so significantly after fifty-five hours that you don't reap any discernible benefits from the time spent at work (Bradberry 2015). That is not likely to be true for all employees, but the research finds it to be true for many.

Commitment to a culture of worth is an opportunity for management to demonstrate sensitivity to the unique character of each employee, including those whose motivation may depend upon knowing they actually deserve the good fortune or benefits that have been bestowed upon them. An example of a kind of inverse motivation tied to guilt may be instructive. War veterans may be very glad to be alive, but they may also struggle with a sense of guilt because some of their buddies were killed in action while they got to go home. This is not the sort of situation that readily comes to mind when thinking about management, but creating a culture of worth in the workplace can make a significant contribution to healing emotional scars resulting from the wide range of the human experience.

My experience with pastoral care has given me an even deeper understanding on this issue. Any number of people dealing with grief would say that sometimes going to work can be a blessing because it gets their mind off their problems, maybe from the loss of a loved one, the deterioration of their marriage, dealing with debilitating disease, or the fear associated with a discouraging prognosis. And if going to work not only serves as a distraction but also reinforces their sense of dignity and personal worth, surviving the immediate crisis becomes easier, brightening outlooks.

Some of us go through life with a simplistic view that what you see is what you get. I may have thought so until I became a priest. I then began to learn more of what was really going on in people's lives. After a while I was absolutely overwhelmed with the fact that these people were carrying on seemingly 'normal lives' notwithstanding the burdens they carried. A friend of mine said to me one day, "You know, Richard, when we were growing up, we thought everybody was normal like us. It didn't take me too long to figure out that's not true. A lot of people have huge problems, and I'm amazed that they can even get to work."

It's not just war veterans, diseased, terminal, or grieving individuals who might be glad to be able to go to work and enter into an orderly, positive, managed environment. It's people facing financial pressure, sibling rivalry, or other human problems—not just major crises but daily annoyances and nagging concerns.

Entering into a well-managed work environment can actually be something of an inspiration, helping employees to develop a higher aspiration in how they might relate to others. This type of environment aids in developing habits that will serve people well, not only at work but in civic life. Sometimes the interpersonal skills learned at work can help in family relationships too.

Work environments can reflect needed routine and space, such as a chair that's yours, your own desk, or a designated parking spot. Work life becomes orderly for the individual in ways his/her personal life may not be. This in itself can be a basis for hope that things can be different elsewhere.

DISCUSSION QUESTIONS

1. What in your own experience has given you a sense of worth at work?
2. What has diminished your sense of worth there?
3. What actions do you take or can you take to contribute to a culture of worth where you work?

Phrases that reflect a people-focused approach to management include "I'm glad you're taking some time off" and "Please let me know if you have any needs or questions while you're away."

Creating a culture of worth helps activate human capital.

7

CREATE A CULTURE OF HOPE

A leader's role is to raise people's aspirations for what they can become and to release their energies so they will try to get there.

—David Gergen

THE JULY–AUGUST 2013 edition of *Harvard Business Review* included an article asking, "Is it better to be loved or feared?" The article reported that the chances of a manager who is strongly disliked being considered a good leader are only about one in two thousand and concludes that warmth trumps strength. Sharon Dauk, a member of the Harvard Business School's Executive Education Coach/ Facilitation team says the "soft" side of servant leadership is now being embraced more widely in business. This is due, in part, to what behavioral economists have demonstrated: judgments of trustworthiness generally lead to significantly higher economic gains. Dauk's implicit assumption is that warmth leads to trust, but I would add that is also helps to create a culture of hope.

For example, Patagonia is famous for treating employees well, and they in turn respond with tremendous loyalty. Even though customers pay more for similar products they could buy elsewhere, the company believes that reputation of being a quality company with regard for people nets more in profits than the industry average.

Trust generally supports and sustains a sense of hope, which is one of the reasons I like Dean Craig Van Slyke's emphasis on trust-based leadership. (Dean Van Slyke is the Dean of the W. A. Franke College of Business at Northern Arizona University.)

> Van Slyke uses an example about his assistant to illustrate the tremendous across-the-board value of trust. If he asks her to make an appointment for a woman who will be coming in, she doesn't instantly rush to judgment that he is interviewing people he might hire to replace her. If she didn't trust him, she could easily spend time asking other staff members if they've heard he is dissatisfied with her work. That distracts two employees. In addition, he doesn't have to wonder if she will actually set up that appointment and waste time checking with her for confirmation. They trust one another. Things get done in a smooth manner, and time isn't wasted, nor is stress created in either one of them.

One company in need of better relations between management and workers created a group of fifteen members. The team consisted of personnel from all levels of the hierarchy, and they set up a brainstorming session with only one ground rule—that unless everyone was in agreement, no idea was put into practice. Feeling that their opinions truly did matter, team members listened, interacted, and ironed out morale problems.

Three sixty-reviews allow for multi-source assessment regarding an employee's performance, from coworkers at different levels within an organization. This process, while not without its flaws, can be a valuable tool with insights and constructive suggestions sourced from subordinates, colleagues, and managers.

People need to look forward to something or have a sense of hope. Most look forward to an improvement in their financial condition. Indeed, hope can be related to ambition, but even for those who lack ambition, hope is essential—perhaps even more important for the ambitious. For those who feel they are living at the subsistence level (i.e., for those who are in poverty), work can be drudgery because poverty often includes a host of other challenges. Yet it is the journey through adversity that opens the door to a culture of hope. Managers should be able to acknowledge the human condition when analyzing what motivates employees to greater performance. For example, public school teachers must deal with students with behavioral problems, which often stem from a host of problems in the home. Supervisors must understand those pressures on the teachers. Likewise, many adults bring their personal problems to work. Employees often face fear, scarcity, financial struggles, illness, and broken relationships—setbacks of all kinds. Yet even with these trials, people still show up for work and usually bring with them at least some vague sense that things could be better. They bring either a sense of hope, or a desire for hope that progress can be made. Wise employers should foster that hope and care enough about their staff to always do so.

Enlightened employers may, to some degree, be aware of most problems their employees face, maybe not individually but in general and at least categorically. This awareness goes a long way toward explaining why employer-sponsored health plans developed, why child care at the workplace is more available now, why paternal leave is now becoming more commonplace, and why behavioral counseling is often available, most often through company health plans but sometimes even on site. In some cases, "industrial" chaplains have been provided at factories (most of these have also been trained as behavioral counselors).

I was told that certain members of the American Management Association are widely predicting 50 percent of all jobs will be short-duration jobs of two years or less by 2020. Furthermore, it is assumed that millennials are likely to change jobs frequently. Managers may assume these dynamics will lessen the importance of fostering hope in the workplace. But consider these findings:

- Only 26 percent of millennials feel like job-hopping is the best way to advance their careers (Harrington et al. 2015).
- About 83 percent of millennials say they prefer to work for one company for a long time (EdAssist).
- More than half of millennials believe they will remain at their current job for at least four years, and perhaps until retirement (Ed Assist).
- Only a quarter of millennials have had more than four jobs in the last decade (Clark University 2014).

If these numbers are an anomaly and people do end up moving from lily pad to lily pad, the vocational track will be harder to identify. Some employers are enticing people into short-term jobs by promising the experience and training needed to move on to the next job to which the employee aspires. In some cases, short-term jobs may actually be quite coherent with an employee's desire for growth (one of the human needs for fulfillment).

Most people also hope for more compensation. Historically, increases in compensation have generally been associated with

longevity and seniority, sometimes without a demonstration of superior performance. If that's the culture, outstanding performers
sometimes feel their own superior performance will not be immediately rewarded, and sometimes not even acknowledged.

> I know one young woman working at an institution of
> higher learning who wanted to attend a course she felt
> would be very helpful in taking her work to the next
> level. Her supervisor refused, saying someone who had
> been in the department longer had not yet taken such
> a course. This had no relevance to the eager employee;
> why should her growth and advancement be linked to
> anyone else who simply may have been hired earlier
> on the timeline? The young woman eventually moved
> to another job where the employer was open to pro-
> fessional development for the staff.

In such cases, when looking ahead, outstanding performers reason they will have to wait too long for the rewards they feel they
have already earned. Therefore, many look for move upward or at
least lateral moves as a way of increasing their income levels faster.
Lawyers I know have shared the observation that, looking back on
three or four lateral moves, they bettered themselves financially
with every move. That does not reflect well on management in
the firms they left and speaks to the lack of strategic planning for a
profitable future.

Sometimes cost-cutting moves not only decimate hope for financial gains but prove short sighted in terms of long-term effects.

> One young woman worked for a public agency that
> went into a hiring freeze and budget cuts right be-
> fore an enormous ice storm and right after a change

in general manager. On the day of the ice storm, all staff got a call saying "essential personnel only, please report for duty." The woman was new enough to her work at the time that she didn't understand this was an operational term and not a value judgment, so she was hurt when her manager forwarded it to her, saying, "Stay home." The manager may have made the right decision, but the employee was unclear about her role in relation to the "essential personnel" determination. The following week at a staff retreat the new general manager brought up the day of the ice storm as an example of how everyone should really keep their egos in check because most of them weren't called into work as essential staff. Perhaps that was an attempt to explain the term "essential personnel." However, this staff was trying to work in an atmosphere of budget cuts, the remnants of a freak storm, leadership change, and a change in software that was dropping calls for service, so the agency was facing an enormous public outcry. Everyone was stressed. None of this was acknowledged; the staff members were simply exhorted to do their work and not to think too much of themselves. That attitude trickled down through the ranks of management. The next spring the agency was forced into paying more to their union workers who were complaining of low morale.

Hope is fragile, particularly when it is tied to an impression of self-worth related to what is said and done by managers at work. Most employees can take constructive criticism. But, an arrogant disregard of an employee's feelings is never on a list of best management practices.

Companies are justifiably concerned about the potential for employees leaving after having received training and/or education that helps employees develop professionally. Sometimes that concern is used as an excuse for not offering professional development assistance in the first place. However, that choice is the wrong choice for maximizing productivity, efficiency, and profitability. As one HR director said, "Whenever I am asked 'What if we provide the training and the people leave?' I always say, 'What if we don't provide the training and the people stay?'" Companies need employees and managers who see value in staying. Often that is linked to the potential for advancement. Training for advancement reduces employee turnover and reduces or eliminates the associated expense of turnover. It also supports a vision of self-worth.

Let's face it. A change in life circumstances can cause even the most loyal employee to leave, and attrition will never be zero, but in general, a reduction in turnover is a highly desirable goal for any company. Even small companies benefit from the institutional memory of employees who recall the details of a negotiations, contracts, transactions, or marketing experiences.

Managers who supervise employees without historical insight into company operations are often managing persons who are ill equipped to perform at their personal best as they lack the experience needed. In some instances, new employees are so unprepared to be immediately productive that more seasoned employees are even reluctant to work with them. This then delays the learning curve for new employees. While not saying new employees are always a problem, there is a cost to employee turnover, usually in loss of productivity and therefore profitability.

There are as many responses to reading this material as there are readers. Some want to do what is best for everyone because it makes them feel better; others are skeptical that being nice pays off or is even professional. For that second group, here are some numbers to consider on the subject of why it is actually in an employer's advantage to treat people well:

> Bloomberg BNA estimated the annual cost of employee turnover to be $11 billion. Columbia University put the cost of replacing a lost employee at 150 percent of his or her annual salary. And the main factor in workplace discontent, according to Gallup, is not wages, benefits, or hours; it's the boss. In fact, Randstad Solutions, an employee placement service, determined that almost 30 percent of workers would choose a better boss over making $5,000 more each year!

Creating a culture of hope should give managers a more informed, better-oriented workforce with which to deal, making for a significant business asset. A knowledgeable workforce well oriented to the mission of an organization will create the potential for the competitive edge in that organization's marketplace. To get there, employees must want to stay put, and that desire is often linked to a vision for personal advancement in the company. It should also help instill loyalty if the company provides at least a modicum of the support services employees need to stay on the job without succumbing to challenges presented by personal circumstances outside of work.

There may be an opportunity to use big data in creating a culture of hope. The use of assessment tools is commonplace now when placing employees into initial jobs with a firm, but not much is being done to predict performance beyond that point. In fact, many firms involved in analytics will confess their assessment tools aren't really designed to forecast future performance and should not be expected to. Moreover, people interviewed for this book who help businesses trying to understand how to use analytics explain that assessment tools are not often used with people who have been with the company for some period of time, say, five or ten years. If and when assessment tools become more effective at forecasting performance, it may be possible to use data to help people plan their careers and predict who will and should be cultivated/trained for increased responsibility. While some employees may test out of upward mobility using these techniques, if the assessments are used properly, staff will know they can look forward to opportunities for development and hopefully, to developing to their maximum capacity. While there can be no guarantee of future appointment to a given responsibility or increased future compensation, the idea here is to give people a reasonable expectation that they will be treated fairly and if they earn it, rewarded. This alone would illustrate management's commitment to the People-Focused Principles of Management.

Why do some companies fail to create a culture of hope? There can be many reasons, but perhaps chief among them is that failing is characterized as a disaster instead of a constructive event. Some managers congratulate their staff on both successes and failures, acknowledging the valuable lessons in both. That is good business practice. There's an old adage—"If you aren't failing, you aren't trying anything new." No one would want as a mission statement "We don't try anything new."

What is counterproductive about a culture of fear instead of a culture of hope? Is there any way to justify a culture of fear?

DISCUSSION QUESTIONS

1. What are some examples in your own experience when you personally developed a sense of hope in response to an action by management?
2. What actions substantially reduced your hope for your future with your employer?
3. How important is trust to you?
4. Why is compassion a necessary reality in the workplace?
5. What costs do you associate with compassion? Why?
6. What is the transgression in not acknowledging human needs and limitations?
7. What do you or can you do to offer a sense of hope or increased hope to a subordinate, colleague, or even management above your position?

Hope for an improved workplace can be generated by something as simple as saying, "Here's what we learned from this ..."

Creating a culture of hope will help activate human capital.

8

REWARD PERFORMANCE

Keep your eyes open and try to catch people in your company doing something right, then praise them for it.

—Tom Hopkins

People may take a job for more money, but they often leave it for more recognition.

—Bob Nelson

CLOSELY RELATED TO creating a culture of hope is the people-focused principle of rewarding performance. Arguably, this principle should not require much commentary. Employers routinely look for ways to incentivize performance on the part of every person in the organization. Sometimes negative incentives are utilized, but they are ultimately unsuccessful in unleashing every bit of employee ingenuity, creativity, imagination, and productivity. Negative incentives operate on the fear principle. Admittedly, fear does motivate much of human behavior, and fear can temporarily motivate employees to greater effort—but only to a point. That point is the level of performance required to avoid the penalties that may exist. Negative incentives do not spur people to a performance level that exceeds the minimum requirement.

Active commendation can be as effective, sometimes more effective, as compensation incentives, as the chapter-heading quote from Bob Nelson suggests.

> When a young woman in the television series *Mad Men* expresses disappointment to her boss that he didn't say anything positive when she saved an account with creative thinking, he looked at her blankly and said, "That's what the money is for." Too many bosses feel that way; if we're putting money into your account, what more could you possibly want? Managers should know and expect that paying positive attention to others actually has a reciprocal effect on the giver and the receiver, and it is a positive one.

Positive incentives should include making the personalized effort required to identify a vocational track for everyone in the company, for every pay grade. That is to say, the vocational track is not merely a concern for rank-and-file employees. It is also a concern for middle managers and senior executives. Their tenure is often surprisingly short.

> Pete Wilson from Control Data stated that during his tenure with the company, management did not promote vertically within a division at the time; people were promoted laterally so they were given the opportunity to learn something new. This created a positive incentive for the employee and a win for the company

in creating greater expertise from within and potentially greater employee loyalty.

Sometimes, it can be an unexpected gesture that makes all the difference.

> The CEO of BW Papersytems in Phillips, Wisconsin, owned a bright yellow Chevy SSR. He learned that being given the car to drive for a week as recognition for a job particularly well done had an amazing effect on employees. He found this practice so successful, he now ships the Chevy around the country to extend that positive attention. Years afterward, many employees cited that experience as a joyful highlight of their employment.
>
> "It's nice to know I made a difference," said Richard Pike, an assembler and machine tester. "A year later, I think about [the recognition], and I come in every day, and try to be the person they think I am."

Find your individual way of recognizing an employee. Some employees like a wall of fame in the reception area; others don't care about that form of recognition. But it's worth doing for those who will feel more a part of the workplace, and it shows clients that the employer takes pride in workers.

Sharon Dauk, the executive coach cited in chapter 7, talks about people she calls "tip of the spear" workers—those who are highly competitive. They don't play well with others, hammer out compromises, bring out the best in others, or form alliances. What they do like is to win. They compete against their coworkers to do more, do better. Dauk says this isn't a bad thing; companies need these individuals. But, they should be placed in positions where they can shine, like sales, development, or fundraising, rather than in human resources, management, or training. Having their picture on the lobby wall with other employees would mean nothing to them without some sort of distinction. A line in an employee newsletter listing them as top performer of the month would mean a great deal. It is Sharon's overriding belief that if leaders would simply take time to learn what matters to each person they manage or influence, and then really take that into consideration, they would be much more successful communicators, managers, and leaders.

Proper mentoring gives people a sense of self-worth and also helps them identify the potential rewards for outstanding performance. Coaching can also help. These observations are as important to short-term employees as to those expecting permanent employment. People are accepting short-term employment precisely because of the opportunity to get education and training for advancement to the next level of another organization. At the end of short-term employment contracts, enlightened HR departments will not only offer congratulations and assistance with transitions out of a company but remain in contact with former employees.

Positive incentives are not one size fits all. Another benefit to a manager meeting with every employee is discovering which incentives appeal strongly to whom. However, management may be constrained in its ability to customize incentives, and the end result could appear or actually be unfair in some respects. But knowing what motivates employees is usable information, such as the statistics below suggest:

- Employees who are very satisfied with their benefits are almost four times more likely to be very satisfied with their jobs (MetLife).

- Four in five employees want benefits or perks more than a pay raise (Glassdoor 2015).
- When asked, 62 percent of employees said they would leave a job for better benefits (Ball 2015).
- Half of US employees cite benefits as an important reason they stay with their current employer (MetLife).
- According to one study, policies that would reduce voluntary turnover include: flexible schedules (51 percent), increased recognition (awards, cash incentives, company trips) (50 percent), and acting on employee feedback (48 percent) (*CareerBuilder 2013*). The same study reports the most desired employee perks are half-day Fridays and casual dress.
- Another study indicates that retirement plans, flexible hours, and time off rank well ahead of fitness centers and day care (Glassdoor 2015).

While the military uses both positive and negative incentives, and necessarily so, its use of positive incentives is especially noteworthy. I experienced military leadership that rewarded outstanding performers without personnel having to apply for a benefit, an increase in salary, an increase in grade or rank, or some other recognition (like a service medal). The civilian world often depends upon people to self-select or self-promote in order to get attention. On the other hand, when people do self-promote, they are often criticized and judged as thinking too highly of themselves. If they refrain from self-promotion, they may be ignored altogether. The better practice is to measure performance systematically, test as necessary, and then reward performance without people having to compete for their manager's attention.

Some people in an organization may have limited upside

potential for advancement because of lack of education or experience. Still, employees can be encouraged to prepare themselves for advancement. In some cases, a requirement for such preparation can be integrated into a job description. Usually, academic incentives benefit both the employer and employee.

Again, *growth* is a requirement for human fulfillment. Rewarding performance is a way to systematically promote and acknowledge personal and professional growth. The individual rewarded then has a tangible benefit for doing what a person is instinctively prompted to do anyway. In other words, there can be synergy between human instincts and company policies. While personal pride in accomplishment is part of the reward, it is difficult to be proud of your work if no one is commending it. Employees may be left with the feeling that they are not meeting expectations, and this adversely affects employee morale. Similarly, morale suffers when an employee knows that, in fact, expectations are being met but without comment or commendation.

Encouraging people to prepare for advancement comes with a caveat. People who have worked as business consultants uniformly report that a certain amount of the education and training required for advancement should be not only encouraged but actually *required* by companies. One management consultant told me even when educational offerings presented to employees are unsurpassed in quality and are directly related to job performance/advancement, if there is no requirement for employees to participate, those who enroll in courses can be expected to remain involved in the courses for only thirty days (on the average). Management must evaluate the cost/benefit of a voluntary approach and consider imposing job-related *requirements* for education and training where there is an expected payoff for improved performance.

Even when improved skills result from required education and training, there is still a role for positive incentives. If improved performance is observed using the usual business metrics or more subjective evaluative methods, rewards for improved performance are appropriate and should be given. (It should be obvious by this point that the principles complement or work in concert with the other principles, such as rewarding performance, helps create a culture of hope.)

The principle of rewarding performance is present where there is a culture of promotion within a company. Many workers today feel isolated and confined, without opportunity for advancement. This is true if it means they are expected to continue doing what they are doing and they are never offered an opportunity to learn a new skill, demonstrate other capacities, or qualify for a higher pay grade within the firm. The principle of rewarding performance is present where people's efforts are acknowledged publicly (e.g., "Pamela had a really great idea.").

One of the reasons promotions don't occur quite as easily as we imagine is that promoting one person may mean dislodging others. Another reason is that promotions usually mean higher costs in compensation and benefits. Incentives other than promotions may also mean spending.

One company rewarded performance even when the performance was actually negligent and had costly consequences. This was not the sort of performance one would normally think about as deserving a reward, but when you read the story, you will immediately realize that certain virtues should also be rewarded; work performance with virtue can be and should be a very high value in every company. Here's the story:

I remember when I was a teenager working on the family farm. My employer, Morrison Brothers Ranch, had a service man named Kendall Barnes, a hard-working man who had been a self-employed farmer in another state before coming to Arizona. Kendall's job required, among other things, that he fuel all the tractors on the farm over the noon hour, and occasionally other routine maintenance would be required during that time as well. One day Kendall knew that a tractor needed to have its oil changed, and he drained the oil while he put fuel in the tank. When the oil had completely drained, he replaced the plug, got back in his truck, and raced to the next tractor requiring service. When the tractor driver resumed his work, the engine burned up within minutes. Kendall had forgotten to put new oil in the engine. When Kendall heard what happened, he immediately went to the owners of the farm, Kenneth and Marvin, and said he knew why the engine failed. He confessed that he was responsible for the loss. For their part, Kenneth and Marvin were so impressed by this man accepting full responsibility that when the time came to select a new foreman, Kendall was chosen. His honesty and sense of personal responsibility yielded him operational control over every activity, every day. It was a responsibility he faithfully executed for the rest of his life, as he died on the job many years later.

Companies must be careful to reward performance in an equitable manner.

Troy was a television reporter who worked at a satellite office away from the main station. He was on salary; his photographer received an hourly wage plus overtime. Because the two were responsible for all the news stories in a wide area, they often worked more than a forty-hour week. Troy grew tired of the other man consistently making more than he did and repeatedly asked that the policy be reexamined; they were the first satellite office, and the normal wage structure assumed other reporters could take over a story. Repeatedly told, "We've always done it this way," Troy eventually got sick from overwork and had to exit the profession. When performance isn't rewarded, especially over a long enough period of time, things like this can be the result.

DISCUSSION QUESTIONS

1. When has being recognized for your performance made a difference for you?
2. What has been most meaningful for you—greater responsibility, greater pay, or public acclaim?
3. Can you acknowledge that others might answer the question differently?
4. Do you think, as you look at work colleagues you have known, it is sometimes okay for workers to remain stagnant or discouraged in their jobs?
5. If so, when and for whom?

One should always reward desired performance in one way or another. That may be additional compensation or one of the many other suggestions offered in this chapter, or it may be in the power of the sincere "thank you" discussed next.

Rewarding performance helps activate human capital.

CREATE A VISION OF PARTICIPATION IN DETERMINING THE FUTURE OF THE COMPANY

You are not here merely to make a living. You are here in order to enable the world to live more amply, with greater vision, with a finer spirit of hope and achievement. You are here to enrich the world and you impoverish yourself if you forget the errand.

—Woodrow Wilson

A COMPANY CAN activate and inspire leadership among employees, and this leadership can take the company to even more meaningful roles in the life of a community, both in terms of economic contributions and civic life. Leadership can be especially motivating for the potential superstars in the organization who are at risk of being taken for granted. However, for anyone and everyone in the company, *participation in the process* of determining the future of the company advances the need for sharing—for contributing and adding to the mix of activity designed to meet a basic need, serve a public function, and improve the quality of the human condition. Lofty goals? Maybe, but leadership is activated by lofty goals and by a clear purpose.

So why involve employees in creating a vision of the future? Here are some numbers to show a win-win result:

> Customer retention rates are 18 percent higher on average when employees are highly engaged (Ross 2013).

> Six in ten millennials cite a "sense of purpose," as part of the reason they chose to work for their current employers (Deloitte 2015).

This principle is at work when employees at all levels are called upon to lead tasks and efforts, employees are asked to volunteer their opinions (and do so), and employees at all levels engage in strategic planning. While visioning is important, the more important point is the effect of employee participation on the goal of activating human capital.

However much employees might like their jobs, a higher layer of job satisfaction can be achieved when people are invited into a process that will let them participate in devising the ways and means of accomplishing the mission. This idea bears some resemblance to recommendations published in the summer of 2015 in the *Harvard Business Review* from authors who wrote that the HR function is not usually considered when strategic plans are developed. Some of these authors suggested that business should be led by a triumvirate comprised of the chief executive officer, chief financial officer, and chief human resources officer. Including the HR function in strategic planning may also lead to involving workers at every level in the process of visioning the future of their company, an involvement that can be highly motivating in its own right.

What follows is an example of disconnect that often exists between employees who see themselves as responsible for marketing an organization and the other employees who work there. Typically, lawyers see themselves as responsible for marketing their legal practices, but the paralegals, administrative assistants, librarians, IT specialists, HR employees, and receptionists all have a role in presenting the public face of a firm. Such persons will also have good ideas for marketing the firm, ideas that may not occur to the lawyers focused only on their own practice groups. Yet, seldom are the non-lawyer employees of a firm asked their opinions about marketing their firm and its lawyers. It does not take much effort to invite the ideas of others and to consider them, but such an invitation is seldom issued except in the smallest of firms. The inclusion of colleagues clearly illustrates the use of people-focused principles and meets the intrinsic needs of all concerned.

Occasionally, employees may want to take the initiative to restructure their jobs for reasons of socially responsible values, which may suggest a new direction for a company. It can be an unsatisfactory situation and sends a negative message when management turns a deaf ear. Even if management does not adopt an idea, it should acknowledge and show appreciation to the employee showing initiative.

I suspect the example drawn from the professional environment is very similar to what one can see in any business environment. Inviting employees into the visioning process for a company helps activate human capital because employees feel valued. They also have an opportunity to demonstrate their abilities and values.

In an interview with a woman who was working for a private consulting firm under contract with a public agency, she explained by the terms of the contract, as long as she was at her desk, she could bill time to the agency. The problem—she didn't have any work to do. The project she had been hired to assist with was stalled for lack of public financing, and there were a bare minimum of tasks to do at that time. She talked with coworkers in her department, she talked with other departments, she talked to her manager, and she even talked with the agency manager, trying to find additional ways to be helpful. Her consulting manager didn't want to help her because she was making him money whether she was busy or not, and the agency manager didn't want to allocate other work to her because he felt he'd be taking work away from his own staff. Her consulting manager refused to try to find another project she might serve in a productive manner, another way of saying the company did not wish to change course. For six months she went to work without being given one new assignment until she couldn't stand it anymore and quit. Her employer was offered a new direction by the employee, one that would find other work and claim the moral high ground of being concerned about the waste of public funds, but that was not the road taken. The employee involved created that vision on her own initiative, but it was not welcome.

On the reverse side, Harley Davidson says any employee on any day has access to the company's top executives. What a morale-lifter, to feel that sense of being important to those at the top.

Gail Bradley at Northern Trust asks brand new employees to notice differences in the procedures and culture between their last job and this new one, and share their observations. The observation of fresh eyes can provide valuable insight, and objectivity tends to fade quickly as the employee settles in. Whether they bring issues to her attention or not, they sense they are welcomed and their input valued immediately, even during the stressful transition process.

Inertia can be deadly where the pace of business seems to accelerate change. Employees sometimes see the need for their employer's direction to change before management does.

Companies sometimes fail to offer employees participation in determining the future of a company because it is easy for management to become enamored of its own opinions. Further, staff development time is seen as expensive overhead, and if staff retention is not seen as an investment—it may not even be seen as savings.

But here's an example of how decentralization in the name of self-management led to highly desirable results for the company and for the employees involved because it led to employee participation in determining the future of the company:

General Electric was led by CEO Jeff Immelt to come up with a set of changes that would define the company. The result was GE Beliefs, which came from inside, from all levels. The GE Beliefs are: "Customers determine our success; stay lean to go fast; learn and adapt to win; empower and inspire each other; deliver results in an uncertain world." Simplification is now an integrated part of GE's strategy, representing both cultural and structural transformation.

Employees who say their organizational values are "known and understood" are fifty-one times more likely to be fully engaged than an employee who responds that their organization does not have values that are known and understood (MacPherson 2014).

Craig Van Slyke at Northern Arizona University believes in the power of the phrase "help me understand." Whether said to a supervisor or a subordinate, it reflects openness and interest, and breeds respect. Changing minds requires understanding and respecting different perspectives.

DISCUSSION QUESTIONS

1. When was it meaningful and motivating for you to be able to participate in the process of determining the future of a company?
2. Can you remember a time when the failure to ask for employee input represented a waste of talent and valuable insight in planning for the future of a company?
3. What kind of leadership is needed to accommodate a planning process in business?
4. In terms of activating human capital, do you think it is the mere fact of participation that is energizing to employees or is linking the participation to a vision more important and more effective in utilizing the human assets of an organization?

Managers should be willing to say, "Let's do some visioning. I would like for you to be part of our team for this effort."

Developing a process for employee participation in determining the future of a company *will* activate human capital.

EXPRESS GRATITUDE

The deepest craving of human nature is the need to be appreciated.

—William James

Silent gratitude isn't very much to anyone.

—Gertrude Stein

THE PRINCIPLE OF expressing gratitude is closely linked to rewarding performance but is distinguishable because organizations sometimes lack the resources to actually reward performance (or occasionally, offering financial rewards for performance may be against public practice). Usually, a lack of resources for increasing compensation is due to lack of profitability or in the case of government-funded agencies and universities, it may be the result of cutbacks in public funding. Non-monetary rewards may still be possible, such as promotions or prestigious recognition, but notwithstanding some of the data presented in chapter 4, I believe most employees want additional compensation as the core of the reward system.

Even where no rewards are possible, monetary or non-monetary, a sincere expression of gratitude goes a long way to helping people realize that the extra efforts and extra initiative they show have been noticed. No one likes being taken for granted. A common complaint in the workplace today is the employee feels underappreciated. When the employee is performing well, there really should be no excuse for this result. In keeping with the overall theme of managing the person and not the position, expressing gratitude is critically important.

Expressing gratitude is perhaps easy to overlook because of the cultural context in which we work in America. Our culture seems almost entirely devoid of gratitude. In part this is a corollary to the growth of an attitude of entitlement so many bring to the workplace. This sense of entitlement exists not only among rank-and-file employees, but it is also evident among executives. In part, the failure to express gratitude reflects an erosion in common courtesy in our society. Even commercial transactions that traditionally ended with the seller thanking the customer are now often ended without any communication at all. A cashier may just dump change into the customer's hand without saying anything, expecting the customer to move along to make way for the next customer. On the other hand, a drive-through customer may fully ignore the employee in favor of an ongoing cell phone dialogue. A lack of customary manners or even professional courtesy then also becomes a part of the habit of mind employed by *managers* because they bring those experiences to work. I should emphasize this principle is not about demonstrating good manners, but rather there must be authenticity in the implementation of this principle. The gratitude should be real.

Gratitude may be the most difficult principle of all to adopt. Across society, at least in this country, the adage that "bad times make good people" leaves unsaid that maybe good times make bad people. Unlike the Greatest Generation, too few of us have known war or deprivation. Many of us had parents who provided safety, lodging, education, and sometimes, too many toys. Therefore, too many walk around today having been born on third base acting like they hit a triple. They believe they are entitled to everything they have, because they are fixated on people who have more than they do. Celebrity culture shows the ultra-wealthy, and the thoughts, *We're as good as they are. Where's our second home, third car, and annual overseas vacation?* permeate society today.

Because people feel entitled to all the good they receive, it will require a very deliberate and conscious shift to be grateful to anyone for anything. As long as an employee performing a stellar job elicits from you the attitude that he or she is only doing what he or she should be doing and is already being compensated for it, gratitude will not come. Seeing other people as more than fully interchangeable and expendable assets takes mindful time and practice. But the payoff is priceless, in both their response to the change in you, and how you will feel about your employees.

Failure to express gratitude serves no one, except it may preserve a senior's sense of superiority over "subordinates" who the manager may expect to work without personal goals and without complaint. The individual supervisor may feel superior, but the business should not cater to people who want to feel more important than others. No one is well served with that attitude. As the old adage goes, "There is no I in *team*."

Let's acknowledge that at every level in an organization, people want and need to feel appreciated for their contributions. Dealing with people who have a sense of entitlement can be tiresome, to be sure, but people are not robots. At every level people want and need to be appreciated for contributions. Even CEOs need approbation, as do overworked persons in middle management. Most of all, those who do the work no one else wants to do must be shown gratitude for their indispensable contributions. A collateral benefit of expressing gratitude is that it activates collaboration.

So, look for people commending others for their assistance, people sharing credit, and people noticing when a colleague (whether peer, senior, or subordinate) has gone above and beyond expectations in the amount or quality of work performed. Where these behaviors are evident, the desired culture is likely to be present. Thanking people individually for specific contributions is more effective than general expressions of gratitude, but a sincere expression of gratitude by a team leader in relation to the team as a whole also contributes to the desired culture. A similar result is achieved whenever a manager thinks to include recognition of more than one contributor each time credit is given. Such behaviors can have the desirable outcome of prompting others to do the same.

Attitude, like rain, comes from above.

> Past Drury Inn manager Jeff Theiss in Flagstaff, Arizona, not only wiped tables, folded towels, and responded to calls from guests needing something in their rooms but took pride in that. (There is inherent value in a manager knowing every aspect of every job he/she is supervising.) But being willing to do the "low" jobs, Jeff was deserving of the "high" one in his employee's eyes. He wasn't in an ivory silo; he knew what his employees did and dealt with the public the same way they did. Unless a manager has experienced it, it's probably impossible to explain the status gained by taking on the humble tasks.

It is interesting to ponder whether the expression of gratitude partially fulfills the one basic human need for fulfillment not previously mentioned in this book: the need to love and be loved. Ordinarily, one would not expect that need to be met in the workplace, nor would others expect it either. Still, there are certain moments when, in relations between coworkers, exceptional performance benefitting others can strike some deep, almost emotional chord, particularly if you are the one benefitted by the work. Even as friendship often arises out of a common commitment to an activity, value, goal, or ideal, these moments referred to may be the result of a common recognition that an extraordinary benefit has been conferred, or an extraordinary effort has been made, resulting in mutual benefits. In those moments, there is a shared bonding around the beauty, importance, achievement, or other value that was just served.

What would love in action look like in the workplace? Well, I would refer you to the book *Love Works* by Joel Manby. Mr. Manby perfected his management style while President and CEO of Herschend Family Entertainment, the largest family-owned theme park corporation in the United States. His description of love in action involves being patient, kind, trusting, unselfish, truthful, forgiving, and dedicated. I like those virtues and believe they are the fruit of love for others.

I also like the book *Love Leadership* by John Hope Bryant. Among other things, Bryant says in the foreword to his book:

> Lest you're misled by the title and think that *Love Leadership* represents the 'soft side' of leadership, let me assure you that love leadership is hard. Very hard. Being a command-and control leader who issues orders and overpower people isn't difficult, and it isn't leadership. It is coercion.

As much as I like these books and think leadership involves love in action, the principles described in these two books are, to my mind, not exactly principles of management, per se. I am trying to give readers a specific daily checklist of principles (check them off) that will enable managers to do a better job. Practicing the principles will develop competencies in management and not just dispositions.

Love in action may involve a common recognition that an extraordinary benefit has been conferred, or an extraordinary effort has been made, with mutual benefits. In those moments, there is a mutuality, a kind of bonding around the beauty, importance, achievement, or other value that was just served.

> For years Lisa Schnebly Heidinger has done volunteer work weekends at Hart Prairie Preserve for the Nature Conservancy. While unpaid work, the feeling of camaraderie and the loyalty to the site manager are unparalleled among this volunteer staff for the forty-eight hours that they are a team engaged in making something better. Sometimes there are gale-force winds, sometimes rain or snow. Sometimes hauling leftover pieces of ponderosa to slash piles takes eight hours of a Saturday, and by the end workers are grimy, sore, and exhausted. But they are happy, because all have chosen to embark on the effort and feel gratified by seeing results. That group dynamic is sufficiently powerful to bring volunteers back year after year. It feels good to be part of an effective working group. Notably, when back in their home environments, these individuals do not normally work in positions involving physical labor, and perhaps that is part of the draw of experiencing it twice annually. So many aspects of our work are judged in a vacuum, with ephemeral results like increased market share and a more satisfied customer. The Nature Conservancy work described produces a

very tangible result. But the camaraderie experienced by team members is its own reward.

The same was true when Lisa was a television news reporter, on a long out-of-town story like the Pope visiting, or a lengthy trial. The press pool became like a military platoon or brigade, pitching in, sharing the experience, and supporting one another. While there was still competition on the air, it was good-natured among those in the trenches, as it were, and bred respect and regard regardless of affiliation.

Those moments may not last long, but they do seem to occur among colleagues. For purposes of this book, it is probably not important whether those moments are linked to the need to love and be loved, or if so, whether that need is satisfied through the development of friendships or other emotional attachments at work. I have thought about these things and believe it is possible the human need to love and be loved is served, in part, through the shared expression of gratitude. When shared expressions of gratitude occur, collaboration is enhanced.

Psychologists could also help us explore the extent to which an expression of gratitude helps generate, restore, or increase one's sense of dignity, both on the part of the one expressing the gratitude, and on the part of the one receiving it. Anything that demeans one's sense of personal dignity is demotivating. A related notion is honor. I have seen occasions on which one's sense of honor was assaulted through either intentional or reckless public criticism. Those occasions were very deflating to the employees involved; it sometimes took months to overcome the effect of that action. For that matter, these kinds of wounds can become permanent scars. I

have seen other occasions on which one's sense of honor was bol-
stered through the expression of gratitude. A sense of honor does
not depend upon an expression of gratitude, but expressing gratitude reinforces a sense of honor because there's not much distance
between gratitude and praise. Where a developed sense of honor
is present, the culture of the workplace not only has its values reinforced, but the employee whose sense of honor is reinforced may
become incredibly loyal and hardworking (if properly managed)
because of his/her personal value system.

Employees receiving gratitude are likely to be more engaged
with their companies. Consider these numbers:

> Highly engaged employees are 2.5 times more likely to
> stay at work late if something needs to be done; more
> than twice as likely to help a coworker without being
> asked; more than three times as likely to do something
> good for the company not expected of them, and fi-
> nally, more than five times as likely to recommend that
> a friend or relative apply at their workplace (Temkin
> Group 2016).

Creating a culture that expresses gratitude is difficult where collaboration is valued less than competition, performance is seen as
an individual merit, and individuals seek to take credit for the work
of others (thinking it adds value to their own standing in the firm).

> An executive in Tucson found out his supervisor had
> tried to get him removed because his longtime expe-
> rience made him more expensive than a young new
> worker. Clients who were approached and asked if they
> would prefer a fresh face all reacted with shock. This
> man had sent small notes, not for special occasions,

but smaller ones—acknowledging the date of a child's baptism, or some minor surgery anniversary. That loyalty was priceless to clients because they felt valued. (The man kept his job.)

I mentioned in chapter 3 the story of the woman working as a development officer at a university. For purposes of this chapter, I will tell the rest of the story.

> Her hiring supervisor was a very professional (highly qualified), very caring, very relationship-oriented person. When that supervisor left the university, the employee was very concerned because those to whom she would subsequently report were less qualified, less caring, and less relationship-oriented. However, they had more longevity and more seniority within the ranks of foundation staff, and (in this environment where traditional management was the paradigm) were thus much more likely to be promoted into managerial positions. What happened next is instructive. The employee stayed several more months beyond the departure of her hiring supervisor. On any given day prior to her resignation, her new supervisory team or any member thereof could have said, "You have stayed several months beyond the date the manager who hired you left us. Thank you!" It never happened.

Sadly, far too many companies display levels of indifference. "Do more with less" is often the mantra. One business sold three times in as many years endured several rounds of layoffs, along with hiring freezes, no merit raises, not even any evaluations, with managers declaring that "there was too much going on." Imagine the morale for those who remained, fearful of being cut at any time, and clearly unappreciated. It's sad to imagine how differently things could have gone if any manager expressed thanks to those who remained, offered to answer questions, met with employees to express a word of support. Lost opportunities litter the workplace landscape.

An inauthentic expression of gratitude or one that is poorly expressed will not meet the objective associated with this principle. From your own experience, you will know that a bad thank-you, such as "You've had a few pretty good ideas," can be worse than no thank-you at all. Again, the emphasis is not about showing mere courtesy. The objective is for employees to *know* their contributions are valued so their zeal for the achievement of a firm's purpose is enhanced.

DISCUSSION QUESTIONS

1. When was an expression of gratitude especially motivating to you?
2. When do you expect to next have an opportunity to appropriately express gratitude in a manner that may energize someone with whom you work?
3. What would it take for you to develop the habit of following this principle so that it becomes a core competency for you?

A small change in management behavior that could have a big impact might be this; each time credit is given, include more than one contributor in the list of those recognized—encourage others to do the same.

Expressing gratitude can activate human capital.

NEXT STEPS
THE REST OF THE STORY

I have been impressed with the urgency of doing. Knowing that it is not enough, we must apply. Being willing is not enough, we must do.

—Leonardo da Vinci

Never doubt that a small group of thoughtful people can change the world. Indeed it is the only thing that ever has.

—Margaret Mead

I SAID IN the introduction to this book that my first objective is to prompt each business manager to look in the mirror. My further objective is to start a conversation by inspiring business leaders and managers to manage people, not positions. Ultimately, the book should produce a different kind of thinking, perhaps with a different language about managing people. Finally, a change in thinking should produce a change in behaviors.

It is at this point that you, as a leader, must decide if you will, in the words of Muriel Siebert, "Take stands, take risks, take responsibility."

Implementation of the People-Focused Principles of Management may require an overlay to existing systems within a business, and the decision to follow *all* the principles will be a decision to superimpose new methods on top of existing systems, or to modify existing systems.

In this volume all the steps are neatly laid out with examples of how they can work and with examples of how not utilizing them can break down a company, or at the very least limit the potential of a company. The question I pose to each reader is: What can *you* do to embrace the principles and implement People-Focused Principles of Management?

The point of the principles is to enhance the support management gets in pursuit of company goals. Where there is a disconnect between company goals and what employees want and need, the upside potential in employee performance is limited. It is therefore important to try to align through visioning, which includes what employees want and need. Visioning at all levels within a company is important, and it should be a continuing effort. I recently attended a symposium where a newly retired four-star general was one of the keynote speakers. During his keynote the major theme was that Western culture is all about "looking at feet, rather than looking at the horizon." He asserted we spend all our time reacting to and putting out fires and virtually no time finding, defining, and sharing a vision, much less implementing the steps to realize the vision. The horizon is the vision and the steps along the way are the plan to get to the vision. Occasionally we will encounter fires (so to speak) that require response—but in responding we must still have reference to the horizon—not just where our feet are.

A former CEO told me he has known too many CEOs who cannot seem to grasp that their own success is entirely dependent upon the people in their organizations. Your employees are the avenue to realize your company vision. Good employees can become great employees and expedite the vision with fewer fires if you include them in the process of defining and developing the vision.

If you believe you have already defined, formulated, and shared a vision, now you need to motivate the human capital to realize the vision.

The Wharton School has a course in the *Strategic Management of Human Assets*; unlocking the potential of employees is promoted as a way of optimizing the organization and creating competitive advantages for firms. Executive coaching can also unlock the potential inherent in the use of the principles I have described. Certainly the manager's potential is maximized through coaching, but an effective coach will also train managers to unlock the potential in persons they manage. Studies demonstrate that businesses using coaching are outperforming those that don't.

Business success is measured by profit margins or customer satisfaction, but this success is directly related to employee satisfaction. Unhappy employees will not be productive. Success requires more satisfied employees.

If you are an existing business, whether a large major corporation or a small family-owned business, you probably already have the human capital necessary to accomplish the company vision, but you may not know enough about the human capital you employ to realize the truth of this statement. You have the data right at your fingertips to turn your business around into the vision. Let's call it small data. It could be like another business man recently commented about his own company on LinkedIn—"I believed in the principles, and thought that my company was following the principles, only to find out that my own company was not following the principles I so passionately pledged to practice."

How do you avoid this foible? You become your own "Undercover Boss." You have small data available to you right now to identify gaps in performance and the reason for those gaps. Maybe the indicators are low sales, customer service complaints, and missed deadlines. This information is readily available to you, and it tells a story about what you are missing in your organization. It allows you to seek out the department or manager that is struggling the most and gives you a place to begin. Get to know the manager, get to know the people he/she is managing, and then endeavor to know the people being managed by the manager in question. Direct contact will bring the issues to the surface.

Maybe your manager is unable to lead even though he or she is able to manage processes. This is an important consideration because people are led. Is the manager in the right position?

> I know of a young man named Sean who was a superstar as a salesman for a large supply house. One of the warehouse managers retired, and Sean's upper-level managers decided because he knew the product line and the processes so well that Sean would make the perfect manager. Sean took the position, and he failed miserably. He hated managing people. He wasn't a fair manager because his personality was one of a sales nature with a "good ol' boy" attitude. He found it difficult to manage people who were not his friends, and he hired and promoted people who were. This created an environment of low morale and hostility. Productivity went down, and turnover went up. Sean was knowledgeable enough about what was going on around

him and what he loved that he eventually went to his upper level managers and said "I am not a manager of people—I am a salesman. I do the most for the company and myself in that role and you need to replace me with someone who likes and wants to manage." He was moved back outside to sales and thrives as a top salesman for the company on a national level. The supply house reaps the benefit of his sales, and a new manager was promoted from within who had a passion for management, had experience in that location, and was sitting right there all the time.

Now you have a place to begin—as you get to know your people, you will be able to identify what their passions and goals are. You will be able to look at where they may better fit within the organization. Affirm that they are valued, help them feel safe—build a sense of connection. Find values and ideals they can identify with, explain company strategies, hierarchies, and relationships. Maybe their stimulus initially was "just to get a job" and they took whatever position they were offered; maybe they would fit better in another area of the company. Qualifications and skill sets on paper aren't the only indicators of employee potential. Clarify the company's expectations, and outline history, vision, and structure. Describing the values and vision gives your employees a better idea if they fit into the organization's culture. Employees also need to know what's in it for them if they are to remain with the organization (i.e., what the company can offer them in the form of benefits and career growth). Many successful people were not originally trained in their fields. Try to find the experiences and passions of each of your employees and develop them accordingly.

Is your company one that spends a lot of time and effort attracting and selecting talented employees? What do you do after you get them? How do you motivate, inspire, and develop their talents further? I consistently heard from executives that far too many companies focus almost exclusively on hiring the right people and then give them almost nothing in terms of onboarding guidance and assistance.

Employees who are engaged are dynamic, energetic, committed, and persistent. They get fully absorbed in what they are doing and think deeply about their work. They are steadfast because they believe in what they are doing, and they often pursue excellence for its own sake. Isn't this the type of employee you want for your organization? To achieve employee engagement, you must use the eight People-Focused Principles:

- Give people a purpose.
- Communicate widely.
- Accommodate/manage change.
- Create a culture of worth.
- Create a culture of hope.
- Reward performance.
- Create a vision of participation in determining the future of the company.
- Express gratitude.

This creates an enjoyable work environment that is able to meet employee expectations and organization vision. To engage this talent, you must manage their work content so that it is challenging, enjoyable, meaningful and provides some level of satisfaction.

There is a way to do it right, and there is a way to miss the mark. I have offered both perspectives.

I interviewed John Hofmeister, former President of Shell Oil

Company. John got his beginning in Human Resources and worked his way up through the ranks to President from HR—a rarity. In an interview by Society for Human Resource Management for its HR Magazine in 2006, the leaders of Shell had this to say about John:

> The company knew it was the right decision, said David Sexton, VP of strategy and portfolio. "Having an HR person sitting at the highest levels of Shell sends a message to employees that HR and talent and people are important to the company."

Hofmeister is credited as a very good communicator who doesn't allow the company to become too "siloed." He provided a broad perspective and a long-term vision. He allowed people to deliver without micro managing. He was personally very believable, very credible to the persons he led.

I recently caught up with John and asked him directly his perspective on the People-Focused Principles of Management to which John replied:

> "Instead of asking why employees hate their jobs, perhaps we should ask them: 'What do you think it would take to maximize the value proposition?' The qualities of a great company are good people plus professionalism of the financial process. A company must know its capacity and integrity.
> "It takes eight to ten years to change the culture of an organization because of all the new people you have to hire. New and different ideas for management are not exempt from human nature, which hasn't changed much over history. People are still people. They respect fair, firm, and consistent leadership.

"If you don't think of your company as endurable and sustainable, and your people as endurable, you don't think of yourself as a leader. My experience at Shell and GE absolutely proved that investment in people increases efficiency, productivity, and profitability for the company."

John said the values of the company must be well described and understood. To that end he identified seven primary people systems that he led to his success:

1. The selection of personnel is about how you recruit and onboard people.
2. The onboarding process is critical and often ignored.
3. The education process provides the skills, competencies, and leadership.
4. The rewards system provides security for employees.
5. The communication system must be tied to the other people systems.
6. The succession system must be legitimate, fair, and reliable.
7. The overall value proposition is the consequence of the six described above—it is a mirror image of the culture needed to sustain the systems over time.

Sounds familiar, doesn't it? Activate human capital and accomplish your organizational vision by employing the People-Focused Principles of Management.

What if following these principles provides you with an employee of the future that takes your company to and beyond its vision? Would the investment be worth it then?

The Attributes of an Employee of the Future

Author Unknown

- Enough confidence in yourself to enjoy seeing your people contribute and gain recognition.
- Enough humility to know you must listen to others and be receptive to ideas as good or better than your own.
- Enough curiosity to encourage debate over strategies—to better know if you have weaknesses you haven't thought of—or strengths you may underestimate.
- Enough fairness to correctly want the best people to be promoted without regard to any considerations other than ability.
- Enough pride to want to be a good teacher to share your knowledge and experience with others.
- Enough loyalty to want your successors to be in a position to contribute more to the growth and development of the company than you yourself have—to have employee succession add impetus to the company rather than slow it down.
- Enough respect for others to recognize the unique and important contribution each and every person can make.
- Enough sensitivity to realize that all our employees need to feel pride in themselves and their work.

I have written much about what employees need and why you should give it to them (within reasonable limits). Perhaps there should be a few final thoughts here about how to help managers develop the core competencies they need in the application of the recommended principles.

Some objective testing may be in order. Big data obviously has a role in recruitment and job placement. It can also be used to test for core competencies by managers, to see if they are performing as expected by their senior-level management. One consultant in the business of administering tests for the placement of job applicants opined that he could readily customize his analytical tools to test for core competencies in existing managers (i.e., test to see if managers are following the recommended principles) and if so, to identify the degree to which the managers are complying with company guidelines or mandates with respect to my recommend principles.

In the course of research for this book, scores of consulting sources ready to help were uncovered. In fact, I was told that there are approximately 125 companies providing the analytics services of the sort described by the purveyor who said he could customize his tests to assess managers' core competencies. I leave those discussions to you and the marketplace, but I am intrigued by the possibility that core competencies in the administration of my principles can be objectively determined.

In all of this, it is my hope that workplaces throughout America are transformed. It is my dream that workers everywhere will one day arise each day with an eagerness to go to work, to grow in their abilities at work, and to succeed financially and otherwise through the mentoring and guidance they need. On the other side of the relationship, I dream that maybe someday employers everywhere will engage their employees with enthusiasm for the possibilities inherent in the employment relationship and that trust-based leadership will translate to more efficiency, productivity, and profitability for all companies.

So the immediate next step is to consult with your HR professionals and/or call your favorite consultant for designing the principled overlay I have discussed. If you see your company as multiple people systems working together, as did John Hofmeister, you may need some help in customizing your existing systems to incorporate people-focused principles. Of course, it is possible the intelligence and experience of people already within your organization can be tapped to modify existing systems through a process including participation from a broad spectrum of the employee base. I have recommended as much.

In all of it, I hope for your success and for the success of others within your organization. May I hear many stories of such success in the years to come.

AFTERWORD

WOW! WHAT A journey. When I began, I knew there was a need for a voice saying, "We can do better," and that voice had to have an understanding of (1) the issues facing managers everywhere and (2) the options available to address those issues.

This journey has taken me to meet business people throughout the country, people working in many disciplines. They have been candid and transparent about the issues, and they have been direct about the ways they have attempted to address them, sometimes succeeding and sometimes failing. What they all have in common is they want to find a solution that consistently utilized would make a difference—a difference in the lives of their employees and the customers they serve, a difference in the environment they create for that service, and a difference in the bottom line for the employer.

Most surprising was that the bottom line thinking was not the first priority among those who advised me. I believe the best advice I got was advice that embraced a balanced view, meaning while managers must keep one eye on the financial resources of their companies, they should look for a way to serve the bottom line by making the needs and desires of employees a higher priority than they have been recently.

The research brought me to this simple conclusion: in order to be served, we must first serve. As a leader of people, if I give more attention to the people I lead, the bottom line will be served. Employing the eight principles in this book will satisfy the seven basic needs of people, and if done correctly, that result will increase productivity and profitability.

This book is the beginning of my public effort as a voice for the improved management of people, and it continues my speaking on this subject for over a year. I will continue to work in support of a new attitude about how to energize employees. The choice to use People-Focused Principles of Management is still an election (that is, one option among many), but for some managers implementation will require a new attitude.

Enjoy the journey.

Richard

People-Focused Principles of Management Checklist

I encourage each of my readers to use this checklist daily, mentally checking off each principle as it is practiced.

People-Focused Principles of Management

- ☐ Give people a purpose.
- ☐ Communicate widely.
- ☐ Accommodate/manage change.
- ☐ Create a culture of worth.
- ☐ Create a culture of hope.
- ☐ Reward performance.
- ☐ Create a vision of participation in determining the future of the company.
- ☐ Express gratitude.

End of day accountability:

Today I intentionally practiced the People-Focused Principles of Management, and proactively sought to include the value of goodwill, which I will use in all my decision making in the implementation of the principles.

BIBLIOGRAPHY

Ball, Patrick. 2015. "How Lifestyle Benefits Impact Workplace Productivity." Care.com. Verified July 20, 2016. http://workplace.care.com/betterbenefits.

Bradberry, Travis. 2015. "How Successful People Work Less and Get More Done." *Entrepreneur*. Web. 8 Aug. 2016.

CareerBuilder. 2013. "CareerBuilder Survey Reveals Most Wanted Office Perks and What Motivates Workers to Stay With Companies." CareerBuilder.com. Verified July 20, 2016. http://www.careerbuilder.com/share/aboutus/pressreleasesdetail.aspx?ed=12%2F31%2F2013&id=pr735&sd=1%2F24%2F2013.

Clark University. 2014. "Thirtysomethings on Work: Most Say Enjoyment on the Job Trumps Fat Paycheck." Clark University Poll of Established Adults. Verified July 20, 2016. http://www.clarku.edu/article/thirtysomethings-work-most-say-enjoyment-job-trumps-fat-paycheck.

Deloitte. 2015. "Mind the Gaps: The 2015 Deloitte Millennial Survey." Verified July 26, 2016. http://www2.deloitte.com/content/dam/Deloitte/global/Documents/About-Deloitte/gx-wef-2015-millennial-survey-executivesummary.pdf.

EdAssist. 2016. "Millennials Desperate for Financial Stability, in Search of Employer Support to Get There." Edassist.com. Verified July 20, 2016. http://www.edassist.com/resources/news-releases/2015/04/millennials-study-press.

Glassdoor. 2015. "4 in 5 Employees Want Benefits or Perks More Than a Pay Raise; Glassdoor Employment Confidence Survey (Q3 2015)." Glassdoor.com. Verified July 21, 2016. https://www.glassdoor.com/blog/ecs-q3-2015/.

Harrington, Brad, Fred Van Deusen, Jennifer Sabatini Fraone, and Jeremiah Morelock. 2015. *How Millennials Navigate Their Careers.* Boston College Center for Work and Family. Bc.edu. Verified July 20, 2016. http://www.bc.edu/content/dam/files/centers/cwf/pdf/BCCWF%20Millennial%20Careers%20FINAL%20for%20web.pdf.

MacPherson, Don. 2014. "Employee Engagement at an All-time High in the United States." *ModernSurvey.com* (blog). Verified July 20, 2016. http://www.modernsurvey.com/blog/employee-engagement-at-an-all-time-high-in-the-united-states.

MetLife. 2016. "A Global Perspective: Boosting the Retention Power of Benefits around the Globe." Benefittrends.metlife.com. Verified July 20, 2016. https://benefittrends.metlife.com/global-perspectives/boosting-benefits-in-emea/.

Ross, Susanne. 2013. "The Value of Employee Engagement on the Customer Experience." *Inquisium Blog* (blog). Verified July 20, 2016. http://survey.cvent.com/blog/susanne-ross/registration-is-open-the-value-of-employee-engagement-on-the-customer-experience.

Seppala, Emma, and Kim Cameron. 2015. "Proof That Positive Work Cultures Are More Productive." Harvard Business Review. Verified July 21, 2016. https://hbr.org/2015/12/proof-that-positive-work-cultures-are-more-productive.

Temkin Group. 2016. "New Temkin Group Research Shows That Successful Firms Have More Engaged Employees." Prnewswire.com. Verified July 20, 2016. http://www.prnewswire.com/news-releases/new-temkin-group-research-shows-that-successful-firms-have-more-engaged-employees-300220067.html.